# Collaborative Problem Solving

*To the wise people we met along the way.
They taught us the true value and magic of
collaborative problem solving.*

*and*

*To our readers, may this work provide you the
knowledge to launch your journey, and may this
book do justice to the wisdom entrusted to us.*

# Collaborative Problem Solving
## A Step-by-Step Guide for School Leaders

Lawrence A. Machi/Brenda T. McEvoy

For information:

Corwin
A Sage Company
2455 Teller Road
Thousand Oaks, California 91320
(800) 233-9936
www.corwin.com

Sage Publications Ltd.
1 Oliver's Yard
55 City Road
London EC1Y 1SP
United Kingdom

Sage Publications India Pvt. Ltd.
Unit No 323-333, Third Floor, F-Block
International Trade Tower Nehru Place
New Delhi 110 019
India

Sage Publications Asia-Pacific Pte. Ltd.
18 Cross Street #10-10/11/12
China Square Central
Singapore 048423

Vice President and Editorial Director: Monica Eckman
Senior Acquisitions Editor: Tanya Ghans
Content Development Manager: Desirée A. Bartlett
Senior Editorial Assistant: Nyle De Leon
Marketing Manager: Melissa Duclos
Production Editor: Vijayakumar
Copy Editor: Karin Rathert
Typesetter: TNQ Tech Pvt. Ltd.
Proofreader: Girish Kumar Sharma
Indexer: TNQ Tech Pvt. Ltd.
Cover Designer: Candice Harman
Marketing Manager: Melissa Duclos

Copyright © 2024 by Corwin Press, Inc.

All rights reserved. Except as permitted by U.S. copyright law, no part of this work may be reproduced or distributed in any form or by any means, or stored in a database or retrieval system, without permission in writing from the publisher.

When forms and sample documents appearing in this work are intended for reproduction, they will be marked as such. Reproduction of their use is authorized for educational use by educators, local school sites, and/or noncommercial or nonprofit entities that have purchased the book.

All third-party trademarks referenced or depicted herein are included solely for the purpose of illustration and are the property of their respective owners. Reference to these trademarks in no way indicates any relationship with, or endorsement by, the trademark owner.

Printed in the United States of America

Library of Congress Cataloging-in-Publication Data

Names: Machi, Lawrence A., author. | McEvoy, Brenda T., author.

Title: Collaborative problem solving : a step-by-step guide for school leaders / Lawrence A. Machi, Brenda T. McEvoy.

Description: Thousand Oaks, California : Corwin Press, [2024] | Includes bibliographical references and index.

Identifiers: LCCN 2024012469 | ISBN 9781071926055 (paperback) | ISBN 9781071946671 (adobe pdf) | ISBN 9781071946640 (epub) | ISBN 9781071946664 (epub)

Subjects: LCSH: Educational leadership. | School management teams. | Problem solving. | Decision making. | School management and organization. | Educators–Professional relationships.

Classification: LCC LB2806 .M195 2024 | DDC 371.2/011–dc23/eng/20240417

LC record available at https://lccn.loc.gov/2024012469

This book is printed on acid-free paper.

24 25 26 27 28  10 9 8 7 6 5 4 3 2 1

DISCLAIMER: This book may direct you to access third-party content via web links, QR codes, or other scannable technologies, which are provided for your reference by the author(s). Corwin makes no guarantee that such third-party content will be available for your use and encourages you to review the terms and conditions of such third-party content. Corwin takes no responsibility and assumes no liability for your use of any third-party content, nor does Corwin approve, sponsor, endorse, verify, or certify such third-party content.

# Contents

| | |
|---|---|
| Publisher's Acknowledgments | ix |
| About the Authors | xi |
| The Problem-Solving Process Flowchart | xii |
| Preface | xv |

## Chapter 1 School Problem Solving in a Nutshell — 1

| | |
|---|---|
| Problem Solving in Schools | 1 |
| Beginning With the Basics: Defining Terms | 2 |
| A Collaborative Problem-Solving Process | 3 |
| Why Go to All This Trouble? | 6 |
| When Is a Collaborative Process Needed? | 6 |
| The Prerequisites for Successful Collaboration | 8 |
| Common Leadership Foibles and Fumbles | 13 |
| How This Text Is Organized | 14 |

## Chapter 2 Identify and Define the Problem — 17

| | |
|---|---|
| Foibles and Fumbles When Defining a Problem | 18 |
| Putting It All Together: Defining the Problem | 20 |
| Task 1: Define the Elements of a Problem | 21 |
| Task 2: Define the Type of Problem | 24 |
| Task 3: Determine the Difficulty of the Problem | 26 |
| Task 4: Urgency to Solve the Problem: The SWOT | 30 |
| Creating the Written Definition | 32 |

## Chapter 3 Develop a Common Understanding and Intent — 35

Getting on the Same Page — 36

Foibles and Fumbles While Developing a Common Understanding and Intent — 36

Putting It All Together: Develop a Common Understanding and Intent — 38

Task 1: Determine the Stakeholders — 39

Task 2: Get Stakeholders' Commitment to Work Together — 42

Task 3: Develop Understanding of the Problem Defined — 51

## Chapter 4 Image the Solution and Determine Its Impact — 53

Foibles and Fumbles While Imaging a Solution and Selecting a Problem-Solving Procedure — 55

Putting It All Together: Imaging the Solution and Determining Its Impact — 57

Task 1: Creating the Desired State — 59

Task 2: Determine the Solution Impact — 65

## Chapter 5 Develop the Solution Criteria and Select a Problem-Solving Procedure — 69

Foibles and Fumbles While Setting Solution Criteria and Selecting a Problem-Solving Procedure — 70

Putting It All Together: Set the Solution Criteria and Find Solution Alternatives — 72

Task 1: Develop Solution Criteria — 73

Keeping Tabs on Criteria Building — 76

Task 2: Select a Problem-Solving Procedure — 79

## Chapter 6 Define Search Strategies and Find Solution Alternatives — 87

Foibles and Fumbles While Defining Search Strategies and Finding Solution Alternatives — 88

Putting It All Together: Define Search Strategies and Find Solution Alternatives — 90

Task 1: Defining Search Strategies — 91

Task 2: Find Solution Alternatives — 93

The Four Cases — 95

## Chapter 7 Weigh the Alternatives and Decide on a Solution — 103

Foibles and Fumbles While Weighing Alternatives and Deciding on a Solution — 104

Putting It All Together: Weigh the Alternatives and Decide on a Solution — 106

Task 1: Set Decision-Making Roles — 106

Task 2: Determine Rating System and Evaluate Alternatives — 108

Task 3: Decide on the Solution — 116

## Chapter 8 Solve the Problem — 119

Foibles and Fumbles When Solving the Problem — 120

Putting It All Together: Solve the Problem — 122

Task 1: Plan the Solution — 125

Task 2: Assign Resources — 126

Task 3: Create an Assessment Process — 127

Task 4: Review Progress — 130

## The Problem-Solver's Toolbox      133

**Tool A: Meeting Playbook**      134

**Tool B: Meeting Roles**      136

**Tool C: Communication Modes**      141

**Tool D: Group Sizes**      147

**Tool E: Meeting Space**      151

**Tool F: Glossary of Terms and Group Organizers**      154

For Further Reading      169
Bibliography      179
Index      181

# Publisher's Acknowledgments

Corwin gratefully acknowledges the contributions of the following reviewers:

Peter Dillon, Superintendent
Berkshire Hills Regional School District
Stockbridge, Massachusetts

Jacie Maslyk, Educational Consultant
Coraopolis, Pennsylvania

Ellen Percont, Superintendent
Goldendale School District
Goldendale, Washington

# About the Authors

**Lawrence A. Machi** is Professor Emeritus of Organizational Leadership at the University of La Verne, in La Verne, California. He holds an MA in curriculum development and an EdD in organizational leadership. He taught research methods and chaired dissertation studies as well as taught doctoral classes in organizational development. Before his tenure at La Verne, Larry taught in schools of education at the University of San Francisco, St. Mary's College of California, and Sonoma State University. Dr. Machi served as an organizational development consultant in Viet Nam for 10 years. He has also served as a Fulbright Specialist Scholar in Taiwan for this last decade, working in the fields of leadership studies and research.

With K–12 experience as well, Larry worked as a secondary teacher and served as a school administrator in both secondary and elementary school districts in Northern California. He has occupied the roles of vice principal, principal, assistant superintendent, and superintendent. Dr. Machi has consulted with school districts and nonprofit organizations in leadership, organization development, finance, negotiations, and strategic thinking.

**Brenda T. McEvoy** taught high school English, history, and science for 36 years. Research skills were always part of her curriculum. For eight years, she worked for the California State Department of Education, leading groups of educators in improving their ability to edit and assess student writing. She has also served as a mentor for beginning English and history teachers. Participation in the California Writing Project extended her knowledge of writing and the difficulties students face when producing a major assignment. She has worked as an editor for several books, focusing on helping writers create work that is clear and logical.

## The Problem-Solving Process, Page 1

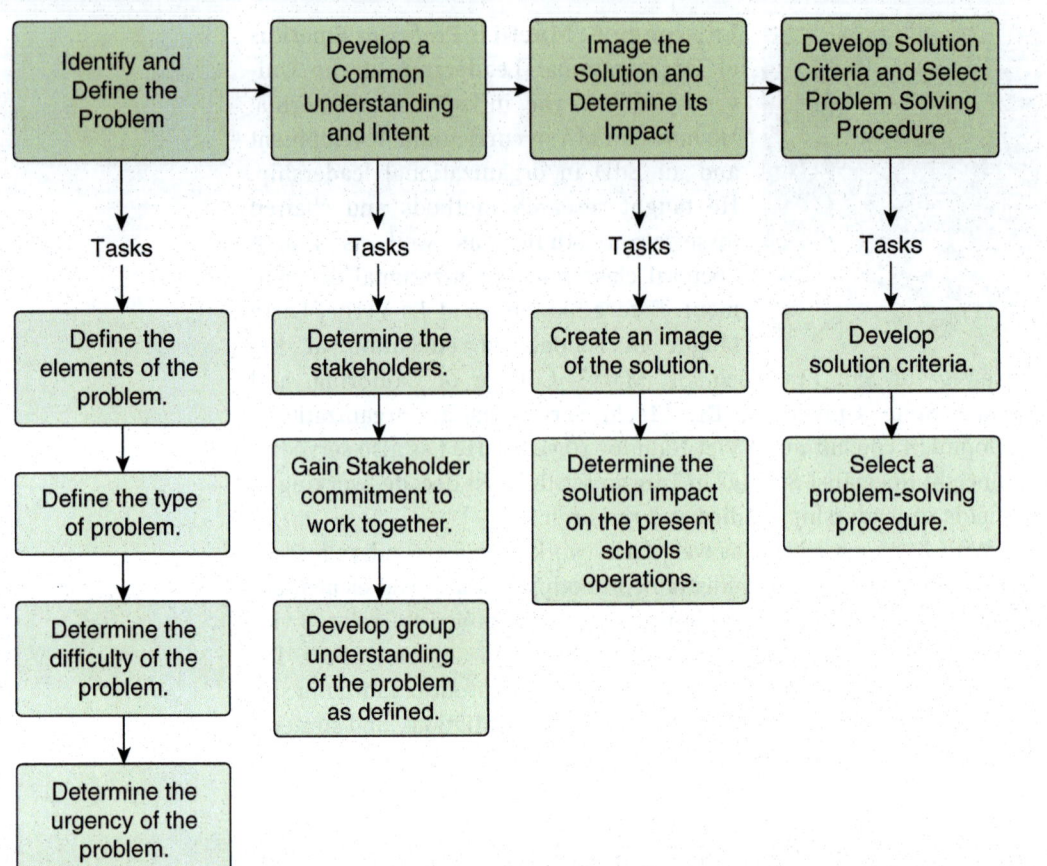

**The Problem-**

### Identify and Define the Problem → Develop a Common Understanding and Intent → Image the Solution and Determine Its Impact → Develop Solution Criteria and Select Problem Solving Procedure →

**Tasks**

- Define the elements of the problem.
- Define the type of problem.
- Determine the difficulty of the problem.
- Determine the urgency of the problem.

**Tasks**

- Determine the stakeholders.
- Gain Stakeholder commitment to work together.
- Develop group understanding of the problem as defined.

**Tasks**

- Create an image of the solution.
- Determine the solution impact on the present schools operations.

**Tasks**

- Develop solution criteria.
- Select a problem-solving procedure.

**The Problem-Solving Process, Page 2**

## Solving Process

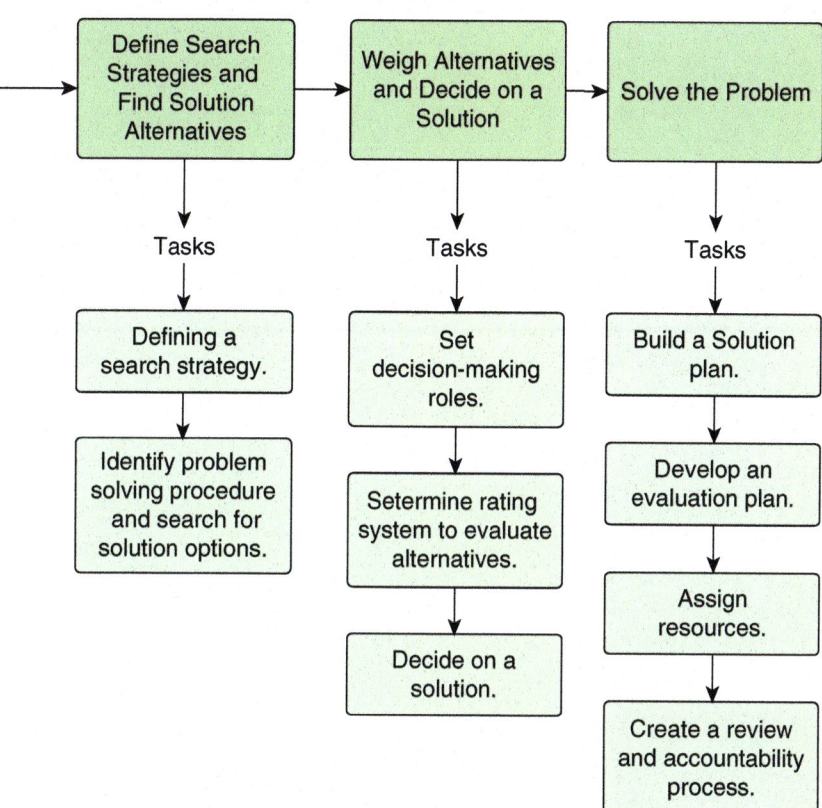

# Preface

In this age of many online meetings, it is easy to forget the strength of using an actual team gathering to meet, plan, and act together to work toward a common goal. This is particularly true for endeavors of importance, such as those concerning the well-being and teaching of our greatest concern and resource, the youth of today. This book is designed as a guidebook into the often-overlooked world of using a thoughtful approach to solve problems.

## Audience

Those new to the world of school administration will quickly discover that much of their time will be spent identifying and solving problems of varying sizes and degrees of difficulty and urgency. A good start is to gain the working knowledge found in a practical guidebook.

In addition, this text is useful to any of those who work in a school community from K–12 to university graduate schools. Additional audiences can be found among those who are currently studying to become educators or who simply wish to improve their understanding of this important venue.

The text will also be useful to those who frequently spend time on school-related business, such as members of school boards or other school committees.

In fact, any leader who wishes to know how to deal with the really difficult problems that appear in group enterprises will find this book to be a useful guide to solving those inevitable problems that test the thinking and resolve in any organization's endeavors.

## Text Organization

This book is organized as a field guide for solving school problems in a small group setting. It presents a step-by-step approach to rationally taking the guesswork out of the process. Organized as a seven-step model, the text systematically describes each phase of group collaborative problem solving. The text begins with a nutshell description of the process. Each subsequent chapter is dedicated to explaining a specific step, from the inception, where a problem is identified, to the final four tasks of implementing a solution.

Each chapter includes a description of those foibles and fumbles that can plague even a well-intended group and cause problem solving to run aground while explaining the specific tasks to be conducted to successfully complete that step. Graphics and charts clarify key points about topics under discussion. Examples for facilitating tasks with a workgroup are provided as task cue cards. These are facilitation lesson plans. They outline the desired outcome, provide tailored group organizing strategies, the meeting sequence of activities, and a suggested timeframe. The chapters end with a suggestion for a metacognitive moment to consider.

This book ends by providing The Problem-Solver's Toolbox, which contains practical guidance for meeting development, meeting roles, modes of communication, dealing with varied group sizes, meeting space organization, and a glossary of group organizing strategies. An annotated list of further reading and a bibliography complete the book.

When facing a difficult problem, you have two choices. You can react blindly and hope for the best, or you can proceed in an organized, thoughtful manner. Successful leaders have learned that trial-and-error is frustrating, time consuming, and only rarely successful. Having a guide through the process will increase the number of successful outcomes, including stakeholder voice and choice, while reducing the stress of all concerned.

# CHAPTER 1

# School Problem Solving in a Nutshell

> A leader is best when people barely know he exists. Not so good when people obey him and acclaim him. Worse when they despise him. But a good leader talks little. When his work is done, his aim fulfilled, they will say "We did it ourselves."
>
> —Lao Tzu (565 BC)

It matters. General Colin Powell said, "Leadership is problem solving." That's what leaders do, day in, day out. Becoming a skillful problem solver is a requirement for any leader, but it is an absolute essential for any school leader. Think for minute. School leaders do not solve problems about widgets. They solve problems affecting people. Decisions they make touch the lives of thousands of students. Many of these decisions can change the course of a student's life. How important is it for school leaders to be able to solve problems? Consider how important it is to have the right solution for a child.

## Problem Solving in Schools

Schools are complex people places where problems come in all shapes and sizes. Teachers and students are constantly problem solving. Departmental, administrative, faculty, and special issues groups meet regularly to problem solve and decide. Some of the problems facing them are well understood. They are the routine problems and are easily resolved by drawing on prior knowledge and previous experience.

Then there are the others, those problems involving many stakeholders, where the stakes are high and no reasonable solution is in sight. The problems Paul Nutt described as "unruly dilemmas with no apparent way out, as undesirable situations without a solution, questions that cannot apparently be answered." These are the *difficult problems* and are all too plentiful in today's schools. These are the type of problems an untrained leader is ill-equipped to address. Having a working knowledge of group problem-solving strategies and techniques is required for handling the *difficult problems*. Not having this knowledge leaves a leader in a vulnerable position, unarmed and unprepared. This is easily remedied. The practical whats and the hows of collaborative group problem solving can be easily learned, and they are the subject of this book.

# Beginning With the Basics: Defining Terms

The concepts of a problem and problem solving are fuzzy terms; everyone knows what they are, but few can accurately describe them. Gaining a clear understanding of these two principal ideas is in order. So what is a problem? What is problem solving? Let's define our terms.

## The Problem

### The Emotional Problem

Problems seen only through an emotional lens are defined as situations that cause significant stress and disrupt the normal functions of an individual. This disruption is often accompanied by feelings of anger, fatigue, excitement, love, or hate.

### The Rational Problem

If the issue is approached from a rational state of mind, then a problem is an issue or situation confronting the individual that requires attention, triggering a rational response.

### The Workplace Problem

An issue or situation confronting the organization that requires attention and resolution.

## Problem Solving

### Emotional Problem Solving

This is an emotional response driven by the feelings generated by the situation. Solutions are sought to alleviate the feelings generated by the emotional reaction, subjugating any rational decision-making. Emotional problem solving is reactionary. Decision-making tends to be biased, often leading to poor judgment, rash decisions, and/or risk-aversion.

### Rational Problem Solving

This is a process of inquiry that examines, analyzes, and concludes with a reasoned decision addressing a situation in need of resolution. Rational problem solving is deliberate, unbiased, and based on the facts as logically determined.

### Collaborative Problem Solving

A conscious act where the individuals in a group choose to engage in a rational process of inquiry to examine, analyze, deliberate, and consensually make a reasoned decision to address a situation in need of resolution.

Individuals and groups can respond to problems either rationally, emotionally, or in some combination. Earlier reasoning would have it that emotional responses need to be suppressed when problem solving. The thought was rational decisions outperform choices made emotionally. However, solution acceptance largely depends on emotional support. While a reasoned decision may warrant the best solution, human emotions fuel the will of the stakeholders to understand and to accept that solution. The head provides the reason; the heart provides the will.

A good collaborative problem-solving process is a hybrid. While rational thinking is its backbone, it incorporates the emotional considerations as well. The following description presents a collaborative group problem-solving process.

# A Collaborative Problem-Solving Process

**Figure 1.1** The Seven-Step Problem-Solving Process

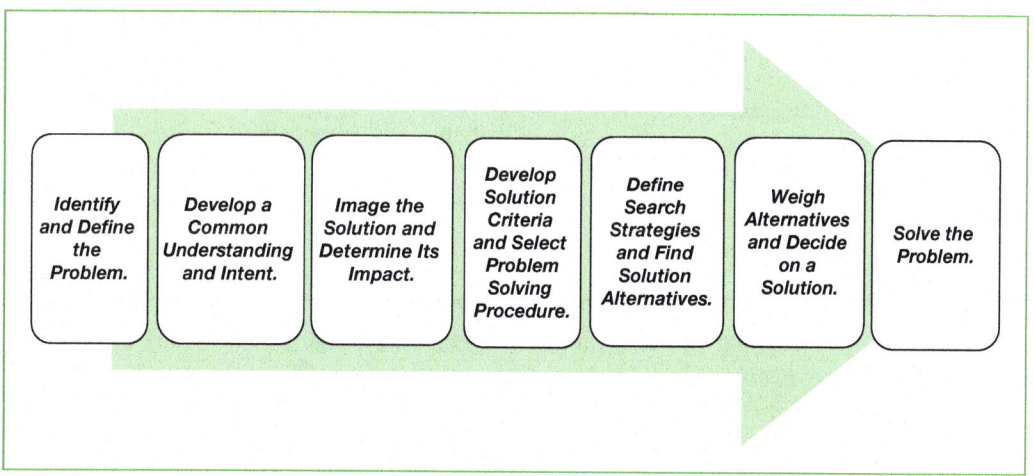

The preceding figure depicts a collaborative group problem-solving process, which involves seven steps (Figure 1.1).

1. Identify and define the problem.
2. Develop a common understanding about the problem.
3. Image the solution.
4. Develop a problem-solving process.
5. Set solution criteria and find options.
6. Weigh alternatives to decide on the solution.
7. Solve the problem.

## Theoretical Connections

The Collaborative Problem-Solving Process defined in the preceding text is founded on the principles of critical thinking described in John Dewey's landmark text, *How We Think*, first published in 1910. The seven-step process is an application of the Kepner-Tregoe (KT Model) employed in government and business since the 1960's and is described in their text, *The New Rational Manager* (1997). See the For Further Readings and Bibliography to delve further.

*N.B. Where foundational concepts are being applied for use in the text, a Theoretical Underpinnings textbox will be used to provide the reader reference to the theory or applied theory on which the concept is based.*

### Identify and Define the Problem

Accurately identifying and defining the problem is the first step to successful problem solving and is accomplished by completing four tasks. Good problem solving begins by observing and reflecting. *First, leaders search for disconnects, comparing what was observed to what should be and imaging the difference. Once identified, a problem is defined by describing the elements of the problem and the type of problem its presents to the organization. Then, the degree of factual knowledge known about the problem and a potential solution is assessed to determine the difficulty of the problem. The final task measures the urgency to address the problem situation.*

### Develop a Common Understanding and Intent

Problem solving in schools does not happen in a vacuum. Schools are people places. When problems arise, people need to solve them. School problems are not "me" problems; they are "we" problems. The next step in the problem-solving process enlists the stakeholders in the conversation. *It involves three tasks. Decide on the people in the room. Gain their commitment to work together to solve the problem. Develop a common understanding of the problem as defined.*

### Image the Solution and Determine Its Impact

In the third problem-solving step, the group pictures the resolution to the problem and the potential solution's effect on the organization. *Two tasks make up this step: picturing the problem as solved and determining the impact of that solution.* What would the situation look like if the problem were resolved? The response to this question provides the frame for developing the elements of an acceptable solution. The first task pictures the desired state, looking at what the situation will look like when the problem is solved. The second task identifies the collateral impact the solution causes outside the problem area. These unintended affects are included as required elements of the solution.

## Set Solution Criteria and Find Alternative Solutions

Deciding on the appropriate solution for a problem is not a matter of personal preference or opinion. Rational decision-making is dependent on sound evaluative assessment procedures. In this step, the group creates a yardstick for judging possible solutions and the appropriate procedures for finding the solution. *Finding quality solution alternatives is a two-task process. First, build an assessment to measure possibilities for good solutions, and second, select the appropriate procedure to find these candidates.* Before solutions are entertained, an evaluative yardstick is developed to assess and judge possible acceptable solutions.

Next, adopting solution criteria provides the gateway for searching out possible solutions. Using the criteria guides, solution options can be categorically identified and the appropriate problem-solving procedure is selected to identify solution options.

## Weigh Alternatives to Decide on the Solution

Sound group decision-making is intentional. Groups rationally evaluate and choose a solution from the options offered. This step is accomplished in three tasks. *Task 1 clearly defines the decision makers and the role of the problem-solving group in the decision-making process. In Task 2, the decision-making parameters are set, and the problem-solving team determines the problem solution and agrees on a rating process to judge the proposed alternative solutions using the solution criteria. In Task 3, the group uses the selected rating system to evaluate each alternative solution, selects the best alternative, and agrees to implement the solution chosen.*

## Solve the Problem

The "what" of the problem solution has been determined, but that is only half of the answer. The proverbial devil is in the details of the "how" of the problem solution. In this last step, problem solving develops the means to a path forward. *This is accomplished by completing four tasks. First, the group develops and adopts a well-defined action plan to implement the solution. Second, there must be an evaluation process to monitor and judge the solution's effectiveness. Third, the necessary resources must be provided to implement the solution. Last, an accountability process is created to include follow-up reviews and reports necessary to monitor the solution's effectiveness.*

Too often program and policy decisions are determined and then shot into space never to be heard of again. This last step of the problem-solving process is as important as the first. Adaptation of this process should always be considered based on the nature of the individual problem and the capability of the problem-solving group. In some cases, the steps can be accomplished in a matter of minutes or hours, and others might take days or weeks. There is no orthodoxy here. The problem-solving process always needs to be adapted to the situation. How is this process used? It depends.

## Why Go to All This Trouble?

Difficult school problems are always people problems. Getting the right people to help greatly improves the quality of the outcome. Including stakeholders in problem solving provides many benefits.

- Stakeholder responses provide bellwethers that forecast the intensity of the problem.
- Stakeholder engagement provides critical feedback for the problem-solving progress and the acceptance of the solution.
- Collaborative processes allow for the "voice and choice" of the stakeholders to be heard.
- Collaborative processes enable transparency.
- The quality of the thought is diversified, allowing for creative and multi-dimensional responses.

Solutions can't succeed when those responsible for them carrying out are opposed. The primary aim should always be to involve those affected by the problem to have a hand in finding the solution. Collaborative problem solving is a must when dealing with the difficult problems. However, integrating collaborative practices into the everyday school processes is strongly advised. Making decision-making collaborative builds teamwork, faculty cohesion, and produces better results.

## When Is a Collaborative Process Needed?

There is no easy, fast rule. Every problem is unique in its setting and context. Generally, routine problems can be handled unilaterally. The collaborative problem-solving process is needed when *difficult problems* arise and *tough decisions* need to be made. *These problems are conflicted, ambiguous, and their solutions are uncertain. These are problems that require action while still considering various ways to respond.*

## Theoretical Connections

The applied theory anchoring the discussions on difficult problems and tough decisions relies principally on Paul Nutt's seminal text *Making Tough Decisions* (1990).

**Figure 1.2** Unilateral Versus Collaboration Problem Solving

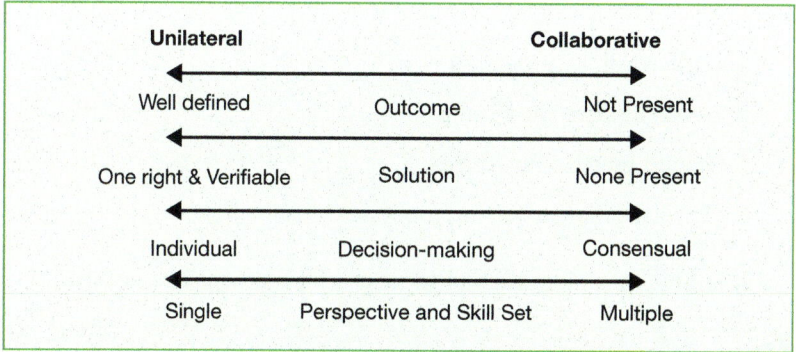

The scale depicted in Figure 1.2 provides a way of gauging whether a unilateral, an abbreviated, or a collaborative approach is appropriate for the problem at hand.

As depicted, there is no need to collaborate when all the following are true:

- A problem and its outcome are well defined
- The solution is known
- Only a single perspective is needed
- Only one person is required to make the decision

A collaborative problem-solving process is required, when any of the following are true:

- The problem and outcome are ill defined
- No verifiable solution is present
- Problem solving requires multi perspectives and skillsets
- A consensual decision-making process is needed

Most problems will have patterns moving across the range of each category. Some patterns will clearly point to either the unilateral or collaborative sides. Many, however, will fall into the middle range where no clear direction seems evident. When this is the case, study the problem carefully; when in doubt, always err to the collaborative side. A general rule of thumb is if a catastrophe or debacle is possible, use the collaborative process.

## The Prerequisites for Successful Collaboration

Successful group problem solving depends on the intent of the participants, their ability to work together, and the leader's ability collaborate with others.

The formula is simple. Tackling the difficult problem requires a leader who can guide a cohesive workgroup in a rational problem-solving process. Four ingredients are necessary to make this happen:

1. Collaborative leadership
2. A cooperative workgroup
3. Sound meeting structures
4. Formal problem-solving processes

It is time to explore each of these crucial prerequisites in turn.

### Theoretical Connections

The prerequisites are principally founded on the following seminal works.

**Collaborative Leadership:** Peter Senge, *The Fifth Discipline* (1990). Chris Argyris and Donald Schon, *Theory in Practice* (1974). Bill Joiner and Stephen Josephs, *Leadership Agility* (2007). Richard Schwarz, *The Skilled Facilitator* (2002).

**Cooperative Workgroup:** W. G. Dyer, *Teambuilding* (1987). Daniel Levi, *Group Dynamics for Teams* (2001). Jon Katzenbach and Douglas Smith, *The Wisdom of Teams* (1994).

**Sound Meeting Structures:** James Adams, *Conceptual Blockbusting* (2019). Peter Senge et al., *The Fifth Discipline Fieldbook* (1994). David Straus and Micheal Doyle, *How to Make Meetings Work* (1976).

**Formal Problem-Solving Processes:** Sam Kaner et al., *Facilitator's Guide to Participatory Decision-Making* (2014). Charles Kepner and Benjamin Tregoe, *The New Rational Manager* (1997), James Higgins, *101 Creative Problem-Solving Techniques* (2006).

## The Collaborative Leader

School leaders tend to be high achievers. They come to their job having track records for knowing what to do and how to get it done. Leading for them is about their capability and prowess; they are responsible. Here's the first rule to learn about good problem solving and decision-making in schools.

> **Rule 1.** *Leader, you are not solving the problem; we are. You are not making the decision; we are.*

This sounds a bit preachy, but understanding the true meaning of the admonition is the foundation for successful problem solving and quality decision-making. Here is an example.

It had always been my dream to transform a high school into a real learning organization. Finally, I had my chance. I had been a high school principal for a scant five months. My mentor, Don Delay, agreed to assist in the venture. I had a clear vision of what that looked like and how to get there. I decided to confront the culture and began to break things. School governance was my first target. It was time to get the faculty to take responsibility for their school. Don took me aside and told me we needed a conversation. Don said, "Larry, if you want this thing to work, you've got to give them ownership. You have to be strong enough, to be weak enough, to be strong." It was time to grow up and put my ego away. It was time to understand that to succeed, **we** needed to do the school transforming, not just **I**.

> **Rule 2.** *You have to be strong enough, to be weak enough, to be strong.*

Any leader's success is dependent on others succeeding. An essential element of good problem solving is having a clear vision of reality. This vision doesn't happen unless *we* see the problem, and the problem is not addressed unless *we* own it. So how does the *me* leader get to be the *we* leader? Leaders have to be comfortable enough in their own shoes to allow others to be "in the room." The leader must be open enough to accept other viewpoints. Leaders must be wise enough to allow others to make important decisions. When this happens, the *me* leader can become the *we* leader.

Experienced leaders understand good decisions happen when everyone works together, and collaboration builds shared commitment to address the problem.

> **Rule 3.** *Good leaders create the opportunities to develop groups into productive problem-solving teams to facilitate quality decision-making.*

It is not enough for a leader to believe and to behave in a collaborative fashion. Effective leaders are teachers who empower and inspire others to become active participants in the process. They encourage faculty and staff to be reflective, to assess what went right and wrong in previous decision-making efforts, and to use this knowledge to make better decisions. They provide the necessary space and resources, such as training and work time, to skill up problem-solving groups. These leaders assist workgroups in team development. They train and practice the specifics of meeting management and problem solving. In short, effective leaders build capacity. They know that skilled workgroups are strong problem solvers, and strong problem-solving groups address and manage the emotional side of the problem. Productive "voice and choice" is the path to good solutions and sustained decisions.

## The Cooperative Workgroup

Margaret Wheatley identified the real problem solvers in a school, when she said:

> History has brought us to a moment where teams are recognized as a critical component of every enterprise—the predominant unit for decision making and getting things done.

Whether it is a school governance team, curriculum committee, or administrative group, this is where the action is and where the real work is done. These are the places where problems are solved and decisions are made. All of our schools have workgroups; that's the way a school functions. However, many workgroups are not teams. They are not cohesive, nor are they collaborative. Many are indeed the opposite—toxic and dysfunctional. They argue about power or status and constantly debate what to do or worse, defer to the leader to tell them what to do. Result? Little gets done well.

If a work group is dysfunctional, team development is the first order of business. Successful problem solving does not happen in a toxic environment. Good problem solving cannot occur without the group working as a cohesive unit. Successful problem-solving workgroups collaborate to develop a shared commitment, a shared understanding, and teamwork when problem solving. Leaders assist them to become teams and mentor them to become problem solvers. This discussion is only the beginning about team development. Several texts addressing this topic can be found in the Further Reading supplement.

## Sound Meeting Structures

Where two or more of us come together, we have meetings. Meetings are an essential part of our daily lives, be they informal conversations at the kitchen table or formal hearings by the Congress of the United States. Meetings should have purpose. We meet to plan, coordinate, and evaluate. We join together to celebrate and grieve. We come together to resolve conflicts, settle our differences, and make decisions. So, if meetings are apparently so essential, why are they so maligned by school communities? The simple answer? We don't know how to meet. School meetings have a bad reputation. Most school meetings are perfunctory affairs, dictated by cultural protocols, and orchestrated by the school's power elites. At best, they are social gatherings, where those who like to meet do so. For many, they are the bane of the school calendar considered as unnecessary evils, events that prevent the real work of the school from being done. Here's the question. Problem solving and decision-making are tasks that groups do in meetings. So how are school meetings transformed into productive proceedings where important work gets done, where real problem solving occurs, and important decisions are made? What do these meetings look like?

The standard school meeting, be it the department meeting, curriculum committee, or faculty meeting, needs to cease to exist in its present form. For meetings to be effective, they need to be restructured. They should do the following:

- Only be held when needed
- Have a specific purpose and intended outcome
- Only include the participants affected by the outcome
- Be preplanned, providing the participants the necessary information and materials to be prepared to participate
- Have an agenda that is pre-published and adhered to
- Be held at a convenient time in a comfortable space
- Have a structure that elicits everyone's participation
- Ensure all participants play an active role in the proceedings
- Have balanced and productive discussions
- Have a published historical record
- Be continually assessed as to their effectiveness
- Have actionable next steps

As Pat Lencioni stated, "The majority of meetings should be discussions that lead to decisions." Sound problem-solving meetings are structured to focus on the problem at hand. Group Organizer activities are completed to enable the group to accomplish their tasks. Each participant has a role in the process, and someone is responsible for guiding an open, balanced, and constructive conversation. Rules and norms are established that dictate how members are treated and how the work is done. These meetings are planned to create a time and space where leaders collaborate with and become part of work groups intent on solving problems. For a detailed discussion on this topic, see Supplement–The Problem-Solver's Toolbox.

## Formal Problem-Solving Structures

As mentioned earlier, problem solving is really critical thinking. The cognitive, affective, and metacognitive skillsets owned by every human are used to carry out the process. Individual problem solvers use the mental skills of recall, classification, analysis, and synthesis to work through a problem. While each member of the problem-solving team possesses the skills, each has his or her unique way of applying them. So when a group engages in problem solving, how do they come together as one mind?

Abraham Maslow said, "I suppose it is tempting, if the only tool you have is a hammer, to treat everything as if it were a nail." This particular adage holds when workgroups try to think in common. Workgroups tend to rely on brainstorming, debating, voting, or asking for suggestions. There seems to be a general lack of understanding of the small Group Organizers and how they are used to facilitate thinking as a team. Even with the best intentions, groups not using good mental processing skills tend to flounder. They become impatient, seldomly reaching the result they imagined.

A critical prerequisite for a productive problem-solving group is its ability to use "group mental organizers," defined in this text as *Group Organizers*. They are the activities and techniques that organize how people think together and decide about things. Group Organizers are specifically chosen to move a problem-solving group through an agenda. They can be a simple procedure like "thumbs-up, thumbs-down," which gets a quick assessment of the group's understanding of an issue. Group organizers can be applied to address the range of the skillsets for critical thinking. Having access to and understanding of Group Organizers is essential for the problem-solving group. While many of these Group Organizers will be suggested in each succeeding chapter in this text, the glossary provides a collection of the basic ones. Texts specializing in Group Organizers are also cited in the further reading section of this text.

> To this point, the what, how, and why of successful problem solving and decision-making have been described. The Foibles and Fumbles section in each chapter that follows points out **what not to do.** Some say experience is the best teacher. These vignettes are experiences the authors either instigated or have been a party to or they are deeds we are either not proud of or ones that left us scratching our heads asking, "What in the world was that all about?" Learning from mistakes is a hard way to go. We hope the reader will learn from these tales and not suffer similar pain or failures. Here are some of our most memorable Foibles and Fumbles

# Common Leadership Foibles and Fumbles

The hows and whys of problem solving are probably the top of the to-do list for too many leaders. New leaders tend to solve problems based on personal knowledge and experience gained as teachers. For the most part, this preparation falls short of what's needed to successfully solve problems at the school level.

## I'm the Boss and You're Not

For these people, making decisions is easy; getting others to "see the light" is the difficult part. They may mean well, but their "me/they" attitude seldom produces positive results. Most school leaders are also high achievers. They prefer to manage and orchestrate situations based on their own problem-solving acumen. When trying to solve a problem, they may create interpersonal problems with parents and school staff. They may have the "what" of the problem right, but they have the "how" of the issue wrong.

Successful leaders know they cannot solve problems singlehandedly. The path to successful problem solving includes getting buy-in from those affected by the issue. The best way of accomplishing this is to give stakeholders a say in the decision-making. Veteran leaders know problem solving is a "we thing" not a "me thing," and their job is to facilitate the work of the right people to do it.

## The Ghost

A leader who remains out of sight isn't leading anyone. A school principal, for example, needs to be out and about meeting staff and students and attending school events. Not being seen, except to those who enter the person's office, means not being where school problems occur. Problems occur on the "main street" of the school campus. They are understood and solved by those who live on main street. To lead is a verb, not a noun. Leading is acting with others. Problem solving is acting with others. It isn't done well by being confined behind a desk or being at a string of off-campus meetings. Peter Drucker said it best, "The definition of a leader is one who has followers." It is hard to have followers when the leader is not present.

## Survey Says

Facts, not opinions, are the building blocks of good problem solving. Taking the polar opposite position of an "I am the boss" leader, some school leaders believe leadership is earned by satisfying members of the community and staff. This means defining themselves based on the good opinion of others. Rather than weighing the various vantage points and perceptions of constituencies to seek a better understanding of the problem, they tally opinions and solve problems based on the view of the majority. Worse yet, they will do the bidding of the powerful or subscribe to the "last in, first out" rule of problem solving. That is, the position last heard becomes the position taken. Such thinking leads to a skewed and haphazard identification of a problem.

Veteran problem solvers formulate a preliminary understanding of the problem before gathering information from others. Rather than rushing to quick solutions, they seek and weigh the viewpoints of others to build a picture of the existing problem. As leaders, they facilitate and collaborate with those affected to build a common mindset about the situation and a reasoned solution to the problem.

### Garbage In, Garbage Out

Some busy school leaders look for the quick fix. Find a problem? Slap a solution on it and move on. Problems poorly attended to have a way of coming back to bite. Good leaders know when problems arise, and don't take shortcuts to solve them.

Wait, there's more. *The righteous ideologue*s problem solve by trying to realize their vision of an idyllic situation and settle for nothing less, regardless of the shambles they create in the real world. The *procrastinators* are those who see problems and leave them for another day. Despite the best intentions in the world, these leaders lack understanding of what problem solving in schools really is.

## How This Text Is Organized

The remaining chapters of this text will address the steps of the problem-solving processes described earlier. For instance, Chapter 2 will consider how to identify and define the problems in a school setting. The chapters are designed to be used as guides to assist leaders as they conduct each step of the problem-solving process. Each chapter will follow the same format. The chapter begins with a description of the step in the problem-solving process. Foibles and Fumbles follow, providing examples of the common errors made at this step. The next section, Putting It All Together, lays out the tasks and procedure for completing this step of the process. The section presents the group procedures necessary to successfully accomplish that step of the process. Notice within this section callouts are inserted referring to theoretical origins for the practice. Two supplements make up the back matter of the text, a Problem-Solver's Toolbox and section For Further Reading and Bibliography. The Toolbox provides in-depth discussions on meeting designs, meeting roles, communication strategies, strategies for dealing with differing group sizes, arranging meeting space, and a glossary of Group Organizers. The Toolbox is followed by the bibliography, and the annotated guide to further reading completes the text. The For Further Readings supplement includes several texts that support or elaborate on the fundamentals of this book.

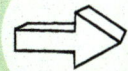

## Consider This . . .

Did any of the foibles and fumbles produce a squirm of recognition? Nobody's perfect, and we have all made mistakes. The key to success in problem solving is to understand errors and omissions, understand what went wrong, and consider them lessons now learned. What are your best next steps after discovering you are in a hole? First, stop digging. Next, stop and think about how to plan for the future.

> You are here.

| Identify and Define the Problem. | Develop a Common Understanding and Intent. | Image the Solution and Determine Its Impact. | Develop Solution Criteria and Select Problem-Solving Procedure. | Define Search Strategies and Find Solution Alternatives. | Weigh Alternatives and Decide on a Solution. | Solve the Problem. |

CHAPTER 2

# Identify and Define the Problem

*A problem well stated is a problem half solved.*

—Charles Kettering (1920–1947)

Most workday events and interactions happen without becoming problems, issues to solve. The majority of these situations are recognized, analyzed, and solved routinely. Difficulties arise when the results expected or required from an interaction do not materialize. A disconnect occurs. "That didn't work." "That didn't turn out the way it should have." What is the next course of action? How can the situation be rethought and reconfigured to produce the intended result? This is the point where a problem is recognized.

As stated in Chapter 1, a formal problem-solving process is "*a conscious act where an individual or group chooses to engage in a rational process of inquiry to examine, analyze, deliberate, and make a reasoned decision to address a situation in need of resolution.*" This chapter addresses the first step in that process, identifying and defining the problem. The chapter describes the four tasks required to build a sound definition of the problem. It also describes some of the common errors made that prevent a problem from being correctly identified and defined.

When a situation is recognized as a problem, it triggers a new awareness. Reflective leaders stop and take a hard look at what occurred. What does it represent? Is it an opportunity or a threat? How powerful is it? Where is it coming from? Who does it concern? Who can address it? How much do we know about it? Leaders, good at problem solving, know making a quality decision begins with properly identifying the problem.

Being observant and reflective are the secrets to successfully finding and identifying problems in schools. Successful leaders problem solve by walking around. They find time to be present in their schools. A very important element of being present is looking and listening for the disconnect. Being present requires the leader to be reflective. Know what should be. Look and listen to discover what is. Look for the difference. Be proactive. Try to find problems before or as they occur. Reflecting on workplace actions is simple; just ask these two questions: What is happening? What should be happening? The answers provide the information necessary to identify potential problems.

Sounds simple, but the proverbial devil is indeed in the details. The following describe some of the major mistakes made that prevent problems from being discovered and defined.

## Foibles and Fumbles When Defining a Problem

### This Is the Way We Always Do It

In most school settings, the staff's handling of workday problems is on autopilot. They tend to do what has been done before. Here is a simple example. A number of faculty members are complaining that regular schoolwide meetings are taking too long. When reviewing past agendas, a vice principal finds departmental oral reports occupy a third of the meeting time, lasting an hour or more. Analysis shows placing this information online seems a better option. When recommending the adjustment to the leadership, the request is denied. "It's a tradition, and we like it the way it is," was the response. Problem not solved.

In many cases, the strategy of "this is the way we always do it" can work. In cases where it can't work, the old fix is sometimes applied anyway. More often than not, a solution chosen in this way is so misaligned that it results in a bigger problem. In the case of the long-meeting problem, not only was there a failure to address the problem, the length of the schoolwide meeting, but maintaining the status quo probably angered a number of faculty members and discouraged the vice principal from pursuing problems in the future.

### I Got It. I Got It. I Missed It

Sometimes, leaders take the superstar approach; they rush headlong into solving problems before really having a grasp of the situation. The administrator is eager to serve. A prominent parent complains that Teacher X is giving far too much homework. The administrator tells the parent the teacher will be talked to, and the homework burden will be reduced. Oops.

Thoughtful leaders stop and think. Remember Alexander Pope's admonition back around 1711, "Fools rush in, where angels fear to tread."

## The Sky Is Falling

All school problems are personal at some level. When confronted by a problem, a human's first reaction isn't rational; it's emotional. Rather than addressing the problem straightaway, the inexperienced administrator succumbs to the initial feelings of fear, anger, or dread and reacts from an emotional place. The response is neither rational nor reasonable. Typically knee-jerk reactions, these responses are generally clumsy and defensive. Such responses do not identify the problem rationally and usually create additional problems. Emotional reactions create emotional responses, not rational ones.

## Too Hot to Handle

Some problems that surface can be potential career enders, expose human error or incompetence, or demonstrate organizational ineptitude. Dealing with such problems is always uncomfortable and disconcerting. However, a grievous error is made when the problem is not addressed in a straightforward, honest fashion. Some leaders find ways to hide the problem. Others find ways to reframe the problem to divert attention from the real issue. Solving a problem under fake pretenses allows the problem to fester unabated. The seasoned leader knows that when difficult problems arise, real leadership requires doing the right thing regardless of its consequences.

Consider this example: An assistant principal has the town mayor's son in the office. A teacher found the young man in possession of six ounces of marijuana and reports he was caught while trying to sell it. Just as the assistant principal is about to address the problem, the phone rings; the mayor is on the line. The problem just got bigger. It's time to do the right thing.

## Ignorance Is Bliss

A principal is deep in thought. This series of workshops has to get it right. Her administrative assistant enters with a pile of papers in his hand. The evaluative reports for three major federal projects are due in four days. Looking up, the principal says, "Thanks for the reminder; you can fill them out. I can't be interrupted. I am sure you'll do a great job."

This leader is seeing this problem as what one friend called "administrivia." Administrivia problems are either ignored or handed off by choosing to be oblivious to the situation. In such cases, these leaders do possibly the worst thing a leader can do—nothing.

Other leaders lack the expertise to address certain issues. Rather than asking for help, they muddle their way through the problem and hope it goes away. Such behaviors either allow the problem to move freely in the organization, becoming far more serious, or at best, they are ineffectively dealt with. If leaders snub an issue, simple problems become complicated ones. Skipping a problem delays the inevitable more difficult situation. Successful leaders know they are responsible for all school problems, regardless of their type or origin. They are also aware when they don't have the expertise to address the problem, and they find that expertise. Collaboration is an essential part of problem solving. Delegation is as well. However, remember when a task is delegated, the responsibility still remains with the leader. Not knowing what you don't know is not bliss but a potential threat.

While the previous discussion highlights some more common and troublesome errors made when confronting and identifying a problem, many others could be included as well. A surefire way of avoiding these errors and omissions is to use the following four-step procedure when identifying and defining a workplace problem.

## Putting It All Together: Defining the Problem

A good problem definition is composed of four parts, a description of the situation, its type, its level of difficulty, and the urgency to solve it.

**Figure 2.1** Defining a Workplace Problem

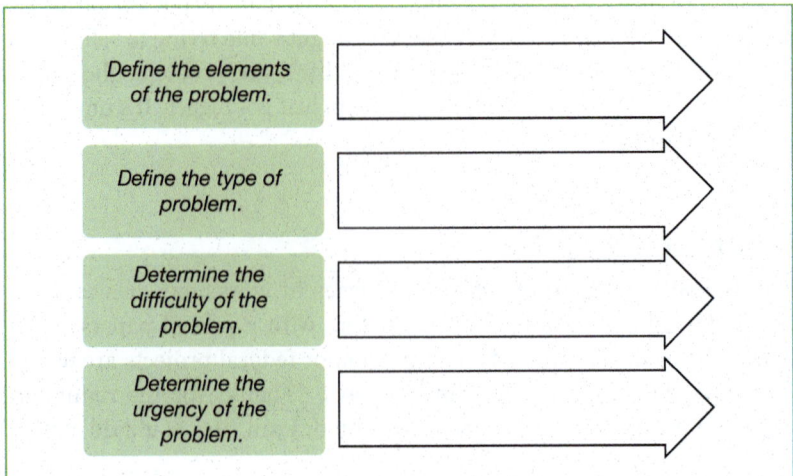

As shown in Figure 2.1, building a sound problem definition is not complicated. It begins by describing those things that make up the problem's particulars. Once described, the problem's type is identified, be it a deficiency, improvement, opportunity, or new venture. The difficulty of the problem is evaluated based on what is known about the problem and its possible solution. Finally, the urgency to attend to the problem is considered. These four pieces make up a sound problem definition. The following explains each one in turn.

## Task 1: Define the Elements of a Problem

When defining the problem's particular properties, the description should be accurate, explicit, concise, and understandable.

1. Accurate means all parts of the problem are included.
2. When explicit, the elements are clearly described in detail.
3. Concise means being expressed in as few words as possible.
4. Lastly, each statement must be understandable using clear, simple language and avoiding any ambiguity. Technical words, synonyms, vague terms, and esoteric vocabulary should be avoided.

The following are examples of strong and weak descriptions of a simple problem many of us have confronted in schools.

- Kindergarten teachers and school aides have reported the morning drop-off of kindergarten students is disorderly. Similar to two years ago, parents are not following procedures and are arriving late. The traffic backup and double parking by kindergarten parents is causing safety problems in the schools drop-off zones. Additionally, drop-off is taking too much time, causing some kindergartners to be late to class.
- Teachers have reported that there is a problem with the morning student drop-offs.

The first definition provides the detailed information necessary to allow a problem-solving team to move forward with a good understanding of the problem. That cannot be said about the second statement.

Vantage point and perspective also come into play. Most problem descriptions and definitions are subjective in nature. An accurate portrayal of the problem is far more likely when the problem is defined from multiple perspectives and different vantage points. The first is viewing the problem from below or as this perspective is fondly known, from "in the trenches," the teacher's view. The second is the middle, the perspective as counselors and coordinators may see it. Finally, from the top, as administrators might see the problem. These viewpoints can differ greatly and provide important insights on the issue. While each member observes the same thing, they often see it differently. The same idea holds true when viewing from inside the organization versus viewing it from the outside. While a school faculty may view a problem one way, the parents and community may see different pictures.

Vantage points also provide a different view of the problem. Proximity to the problem can provide a different picture of what is being seen. If the observer is at Ground Zero, he or she sees all of the particulars. Individuals who are observing from a distance, while not seeing the particulars, will see the context surrounding the problem. A close vantage point sees the trees. A distant vantage point sees the forest. The inclusion of various vantage points and perspectives is important when problems are complex.

Remember the lesson memorialized in the poem "The Six Blind Men and the Elephant," by John Godfrey Saxe. As the poem goes, each of the blind men is given the task of defining the elephant. The most important line in poem tells the tale, *"Though each was partly in the right/And all were in the wrong!"* While each blind man was right, it was only when they combined their descriptions that the elephant was properly described. Vantage points and perspectives provide reference points that form a comprehensive depiction providing more accuracy and specificity to the problem description. As a bonus, when each member's observation is integrated into the problem definition, the group comes closer to a common understanding of the situation. This idea is critical, since everyone should be attempting to solve the entire problem and not just a part they perceive. Figure out the both/and, not the either/or.

## Theoretical Connections

The theoretical foundation for this section is found in the discipline of philosophy, specifically in the areas of argumentation and reasoning. The problem properties are applied adaptations of the concepts presented in Wayne Booth, Gregory Columb, and Joseph Williams et al. (2016), *The Craft of Research*. The conceptual basis for Step 1 is founded on the principles of reasoning. The text *An Introductions to Reasoning* (1984) by Stephen Toulmin, Richard D. Rieke, and Allan Janik, provides an excellent overview of the principles of argumentation.

**CHAPTER 2.** Identify and Define the Problem    23

**Figure 2.2**  Describing the Elements of the Problem

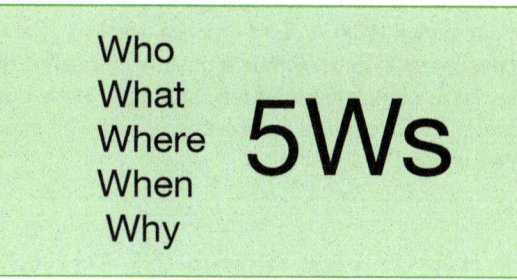

> Who
> What
> Where  **5Ws**
> When
> Why

*Task. Define and Describe the Elements of the Problem.*
Define the elements of the problem by using the 5Ws (see Figure 2.2). Remember, it's critically important to get multiple vantage points and perspectives when creating a problem's definition.

## TASK CUE CARD

- *Desired Outcome:* A well delineated problem description accurately depicts the who, what, when, where, and why (how) of the situation observed, incorporating the most salient accountings of the members' reporting.

- *Group Organizers:* It is suggested that three Group Organizers be used: The *Whip Around, Brainstorming,* and the *Winnowing Process* (for an explanation of each Group Organizer, see the glossary).

- *Your Team Lesson Plan:* Prominently display five flip charts where all members of the group have visual access. Each chart will feature one of the 5Ws. Arrange member chairs in a half circle facing the chart area. As an alternative, you can position round tables, accommodating no more than six people, around the chart area. To begin, brainstorm. Give the members of the group approximately five minutes to consider what the 5Ws describe about the situation in question. At the end of a five-minute period, do a quick thumbs-up to determine who has finished. Ask those still working if they need one or two minutes to complete their work. Once all members are finished, ask them to stretch and come up with two to three more descriptors. Once done, have the group report out the first W—the Who of the problem. Beginning with one member, and then all in succession, ask each member to provide a descriptor of the Who of the problem. Continue *whipping* around the group in succession until all descriptors have been posted on the chart. Conduct the same process for the next four Ws. At the end of this process, ask the group to eliminate duplicates and to combine descriptors where appropriate. Once done, have the scribe or the group develop a written description for each of the Ws using the descriptors posted. You can also use

*(Continued)*

> (Continued)
>
> sticky notes as an alternative *Whip Around Process.* Instead of asking each member to state a descriptor in turn, members post their notes on each of the 5W charts after they have completed their brainstorming. Once posted, eliminating and combining descriptors can be conducted. This process should be completed within 20–45 minutes.

## Task 2: Define the Type of Problem

Begin to identify the problem by searching for the cause of its novel behavior. Problems that cause unexpected outcomes can be placed into four distinctive types. As seen in Figure 2.3, the types are a deficit or deficiency, an emerging opportunity, sequential improvement, or a new undertaking.

**Figure 2.3** Problem Types

|  | Reactive | Proactive |
|---|---|---|
| Urgent | Deficit Deficiency | Emerging Opportunity |
| Considered | Sequential Improvement | New Undertaking |

*The Deficit or Deficiency:* A *deficit* is a shortage of something. A *deficiency* occurs when something falls short of expectation or requirement. In both of these situations, the organization is in reactive mode, needing to respond. Usually, there is a certain degree of urgency to address the issue. Examples of deficits in schools are plentiful.

- The principal is informed that school expenditures exceeded the budget allocated, thus creating a deficit.
- A school board is informed that the tax measure designed to meet the inflationary pressures on current school revenues has not passed.
- The school district operating budgets now are in deficit.

Examples of deficiencies are abundant as well.

- The state has published the school's student grade-level scores in reading and mathematics. The third graders are scoring below grade level in reading comprehension.

- The faculty senate has just received a report. Based on the college's entry assessment batteries, 50% of the incoming freshmen are performing below acceptable standards for entry into English 1A.

*Sequential Improvement:* Sequential improvement problems occur when, based on observation and assessment, better results and outcomes can be produced by making a change in a current process or condition. By doing so, a procedure becomes more responsive, or a better outcome is realized.

Here are two examples of sequential improvement problems.

- After research, the school's primary grades teaching faculty find if they integrate an enhanced phonics teaching strategy into the curriculum, it will substantially increase the reading performance of their second-grade male students.

- The counseling staff of a high school is recommending an online class be implemented for use in spring scheduling. Data suggest implementing this program will reduce scheduling errors by 10% and complete the process in two weeks less time.

*Emerging Opportunity:* Problems fitting this category are situations where conditions or circumstances are present that, if acted upon, will produce a benefit or advantage for the organization. In many cases, these opportunities are only available for a limited period of time.

- Grants are good examples of an emerging opportunity. An elementary principal has been notified that grant opportunities are available for reading improvement initiatives.

- The dean has been informed that with quick action, the recruitment of 40 new candidates for the college's master's program is almost a sure thing.

*New Undertaking.* The new undertaking problem is the building of an enterprise that does not currently exist in the organization. Usually, it is the organization's first experience with such a venture. The potential benefits gained from careful planning would be exceptional. The venture would add new capabilities and capacity. Here are a couple of examples of a new undertaking problem.

- Demographics suggest adding a PreK program to the school schedule will increase overall enrollment. Additionally, adding this program to the school's offerings will increase overall school revenues.

- The high school leadership council has determined the school's academic program will be greatly enhanced by adding an International Baccalaureate program to the curriculum.

## Theoretical Connections

The problem types model described is adapted from the widely used classification of business problems: **shortfall, opportunity, improvement,** and **new venture**.

*Task. Define and Describe the Impact of the Problem on the Organization.* Classifying the situation's impact gives leaders a sense how to respond to solve the problem. Identifying the problem's impact also begins to produce an understanding of the problem's potency and urgency.

## TASK CUE CARD

- *Desired Outcome:* The group should have a common understanding of the impact the situation presents to the organization.

- *Group Organizers:* Two Group Organizers are used here, the *Thumbs-Up Process* and the *Winnowing Process*.

- *Your Team Lesson Plan:* The group now has a sound description of the problem in hand. Place a copy of Figure 2.3 on a flipchart or whiteboard. Review the definition for each impact type shown on the chart. Ask the group members if anyone needs clarification of the definitions presented. Respond as necessary. Once the group has an understanding of the types, ask them to identify the problem's impact using a *Thumbs-Up* process. If all members are in agreement as to the choice, proceed to noting the reasons for the choice. If members are not in agreement, have each member state the reason for their individual choice and list those choices on the flipcharts or whiteboard by impact type. When listings are completed, have the group review the rationale for each type and select the best reasonable choice. Estimated time to complete this task is 5–15 minutes.

# Task 3: Determine the Difficulty of the Problem

Having described and defined the type of problem being faced, determine its difficulty based on what is known about it.

**Figure 2.4** Classifying the Difficulty of Problem

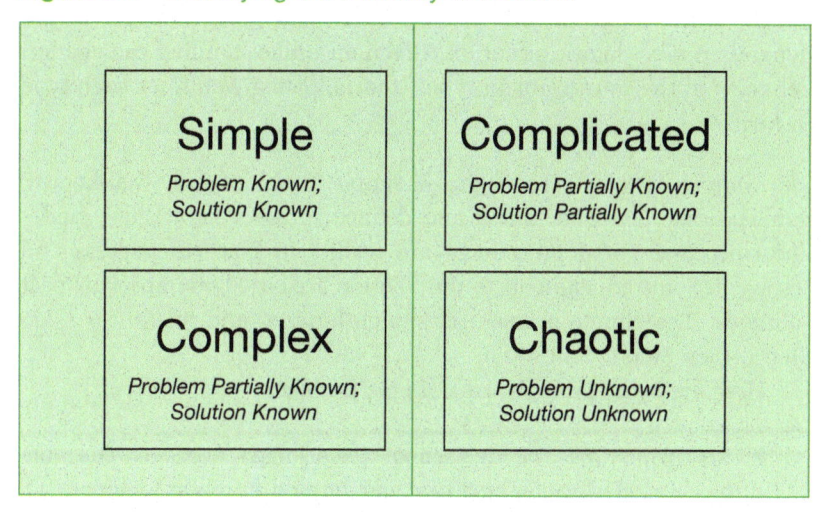

| | |
|---|---|
| **Simple**<br>*Problem Known;*<br>*Solution Known* | **Complicated**<br>*Problem Partially Known;*<br>*Solution Partially Known* |
| **Complex**<br>*Problem Partially Known;*<br>*Solution Known* | **Chaotic**<br>*Problem Unknown;*<br>*Solution Unknown* |

*Source:* Adapted from the Cynefin Framework (2003), Cynthia Kurtz and Dave Snowden.

Cynthia Kurtz and Dave Snowden of IBM created the best model for classifying problem knowability. A problem's difficulty is based on what is known about it and what is known about its solution. The more known about a problem and its solution, the less difficult it is to solve. The less known, the more difficult the problem will be to solve. The *Cynefin Framework*, as they named it, categorizes problem types from the simple to the chaotic, based on each problem's order, ambiguity, and the available knowledge of it. Four in number, the classifications are simple, complicated, complex, and chaotic. *Simple* and *complicated* problems have consistent and replicative elements. *Complex* and *chaotic* problems are dynamic and have elements that are novel and changing.

*Static Problems:* The term *static* means regular and stable. Static problems are commonly known about and have predictable solutions. Their elements are formed like machinery, where problem parts can be interchanged and also improved. The vast number of solutions for the static problem can be adopted from a selection of previously known alternatives. Dealing with the kindergarten drop-off and pickup que is an example of a static problem.

*Changing Problems. Changing problems* are ones where their environments are in flux and/or where the problem properties are in disorder. The evolution and movement of these problems are ill defined. The solutions for *changing problems* are not normally found by adopting previous solution alternatives but are dependent on solutions that adapt to a new environment or circumstance. Staffing levels are an example of a dynamic situation dependent on student enrollment and budget allocations. An influenza outbreak is a great example of the dynamism of a chaotic situation. Given an understanding the general behavior of the four problem types, the following examines each type in turn.

*The Simple Problem.* To begin, a simple problem is a well-known, familiar issue. Once identified and defined, present knowledge, guidelines, processes, and procedures are readily in place to address and resolve it. Some adjustments to the solution are based on improving past solutions. The simple problem is straightforward and linear. First, do Step 1, then Step 2, and so on.

Here are some examples of a simple problem:

- It is spring time. The high school vice principal needs to determine the class offerings for next year and develop a process for creating a student class schedule for the coming year.

- Parent–teacher night is scheduled to occur in four weeks. The principal needs to develop a program that maximizes the positive interaction between teachers and parents.

- The college dean needs to develop the graduation day program for the college.

Each of these examples portrays a problem easily identified, previously defined, and having solutions readily available.

The *complicated problem* has knowable parts as well. The difference between the complicated and the simple problem is that while the parts of the complicated problem are knowable, one or more of those parts are not knowable. So in order to adequately identify, define, and solve this problem, leadership must find, consult, and perhaps collaborate with those who are familiar with the currently unknown parts.

Here are some examples of a complicated problem:

- Detecting recent deficiencies in student learning, the faculty wishes to broaden its instructional strategies. The school principal brings in a curriculum consultant to assist the relevant faculty members in selecting and becoming proficient in a certain type of instruction to improve student learning.

- Colleges are facing turbulent times. The strategies and programs of the past are not achieving the same results. The faculty has decided to develop a strategic plan. The president or dean seeks out experts in future forecasting, scenario building, and strategic planning to assist the faculty in program development.

As seen, in both cases, school personnel have generally identified the problem but, due to the lack of in-house knowledge, must seek outside expertise to help them identify, define, and develop processes to solve the problem.

*The Complex Problem.* A *complex problem* is changing, emerging, and not fully knowable. It is changing because it elements are changing. It is emergent because the problem as observed is not fully formed, and future events can dramatically change its final definition and potential solution. Since the future will form its critical parts, the problem is not fully known. Due to its nature, it is ambiguous and confusing. Depending on its severity, the complex problem can be very volatile. Each of these is dependent upon future events and policy determinations.

Salient examples of the complex problem are the following:

- School closures
- Program course eliminations
- Potential school funding reductions

*Chaotic Problems.* The *chaotic problem* is the most ambiguous and difficult issue to address. It is not knowable, predictable, or stable. Due to its foreign nature and immediacy, it tends to be highly volatile and often creates a crisis. Being unaware of its true nature, school leadership is usually taken by surprise. The situation is extremely ambiguous and unnerving. The staff has no known associations to identify it, and the problem's dynamics are so irregular it's hard to observe it accurately. While the effects of the problem can be seen, they only offer clues as to what it might be. The perfect example of the chaotic problem is a pandemic like COVID-19. The problem seems to emerge from nowhere; it takes us by surprise; we have no immediate solutions to counteract it; and it can have devastating consequences.

*Task. Determine the Difficulty of the Problem.*
There is a tendency for groups, having described the problem, to rush and misidentify its difficulty. Impress on the group that recognizing what we know and don't know about the problem helps determine the correct processes to solve it, the time required to obtain that solution, and the difficulty and the urgency to solve it. A misunderstanding of the problem's difficulty leads to a flawed problem-solving process and inappropriate solutions.

> **TASK CUE CARD**
>
> - *Desired Outcome:* The group has determined whether the situation presents a simple, complicated, complex, or chaotic problem.
>
> - *Group Organizers:* Two Group Organizers are used in this plan—*Sticky Notes* and the *Winnowing Process.*
>
> - *Your Team Lesson Plan:* As with the previous step, explain the task and go over the definitions for the types as shown in Figure 2.4. Ask the group to review the results from the first two tasks. Using that information, determine what is currently known about the problem and its potential solution, as well as what is not known about the problem and any possible solution. Allow members sufficient time to note the responses on sticky notes. Once done, have group members post their notes on the appropriate flipchart sheet—Known about the Problem, Unknown about the Problem, Known about the Solution, Unknown about the Solution. Have the scribe or a group member review the posted notes on each chart, eliminate duplicates, and combine similar ideas. Once the charts have been revised, discuss chart contents with the group. Based on the discussion, have the group determine the problem type. The estimated time for this activity is 20–45 minutes.

## Task 4: Urgency to Solve the Problem: The SWOT

A SWOT analysis is principally used to assess a school's overall capability and is generally conducted when staff is strategically planning. In this case, however, the SWOT tool has been adapted to assess a problem's potency and the urgency to solve it.

As can be seen in Figure 2.5, the SWOT looks at the problem's impact and the school's ability to address it. Based on the description of its particulars, classifications, and characteristics, the problem is evaluated based on the opportunity or threat that it poses and the strengths or the weaknesses of the school to address it. If a problem has been assessed to be a threat and the ability to respond to it has been assessed as weak, this problem is likely potent, with a high need to solve. On the other hand, a problem that can be defined as an opportunity, playing into the school's strength, may have less potency and need. This distinction is important to note when using a SWOT to determine the power of a problem. There is no hard and fast formula, as situations vary. Each problem should be assessed on its definition of specifics and its situation in context to accurately determine the urgency to solve it.

**Figure 2.5** Adaptation of a SWOT Analysis

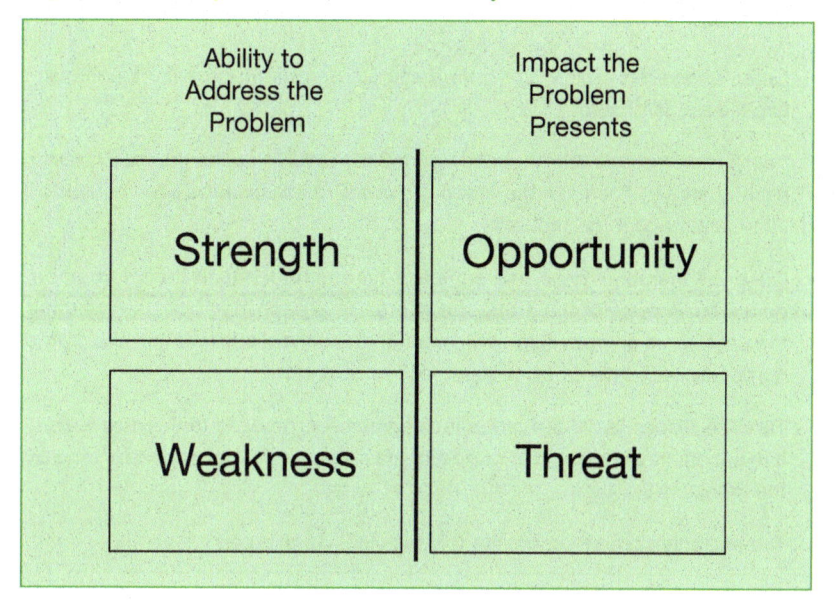

|  Ability to Address the Problem | Impact the Problem Presents |
|---|---|
| Strength | Opportunity |
| Weakness | Threat |

## Theoretical Connections

The SWOT concept can be attributed to Albert Humphrey, who first applied the concept in a Stanford research project in the 1960s. The model as used today was first employed by Urick and Orr at the Long Range Planning seminar held to Zurick in 1964.

*Task. Determine the Potency and Urgency of the Problem.*
The time span for solving a problem is dependent on the problem's effect on the organization. Explain to the group that external threats to the school and the school's weaknesses are much more critical to solve than perhaps the pursuit of opportunities by the staff. Explain how the SWOT works. Finally, point out to the group that the outcome for this task is to identify the problem's power and the urgency to solve it.

## TASK CUE CARD

- *Desired Outcome:* The potency and urgency to solve the problem are identified.

- *Group Organizers: The Whip Around* and *Consensus Process* are the Group Organizers used here.

- *Your Team Lesson Plan:* Present Figure 2.5—SWOT—to the group. Explain each quadrant. Then ask the group members to examine the accumulated information about the problem.

- Once the members have had sufficient time to understand the information, do a *Whip Around* of the group members. Have each member state whether the problem is an opportunity or threat to the school and whether the staff's response would come from weakness or strength.

- Tally the responses. If the group is in agreement, proceed to the next task. If members have differences of opinion, facilitate a common understanding by the group.

- The estimated time to complete this task is 5–15 minutes.

## Creating the Written Definition

*Task. Compose a Written Definition and Description of the Problem.*
Up to this point, the group has accumulated important information about the "what" and "how" of the problem. Now the acquired information will be organized to compose an inclusive and accurate written statement defining and describing the problem.

## TASK CUE CARD

- *Desired Outcome:* A written statement defining and describing the problem.

- *Group Organizers:* Two Group Organizers are used for this task—The *Clarification Process* and *Consensus Process*.

- *Your Team Lesson Plan:* Appoint or have the group select a writing team of two or three of its members to compose the problem statement. The writing team is given all of the information accumulated in the previous tasks. Provide a sufficient amount of time for the writing team to compose the problem statement. Once completed, have the writing team present the statement to the group. Post the written statement on the flipchart. Make sure it is easily read by the entire group. Provide time for the group to ask questions for clarification. Once completed, ask for amendments to the statement. Incorporate accepted amendments, and finalize the statement. The estimated time for the group to review the written statement is 15–20 minutes. This does not include the time required for writing the statement.

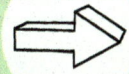

## Consider This . . .

Identifying and defining a problem well is the foundation to successful problem solving. Any builder will tell you, an error in a building's foundation creates errors throughout the entire project. So too with problem solving. Building a strong foundation begins by clearly identifying a situation needing attention. Leaders experienced in problem solving have learned to be reflective, constantly asking two questions: What is? and What should be? They practice problem solving by walking around, seeking to uncover and anticipate problems in a proactive manner.

Successful problem solvers avoid the common errors in identifying and defining problems. They stop and think: They engage others as necessary, and they examine the situation from many vantage points and perspectives. They are rational in their thinking, addressing the problem straight on.

A strong problem definition is built on four pillars: the description of the situation, the type of problem it represents, its difficulty to solve, and the urgency to solve it. When leaders and problem-solving groups address each of these elements in turn, they are able to develop a clear and comprehensive definition of a problem.

Before leaving this chapter, some sage advice for the neophyte school leader. When identifying and defining problems remember the following: Don't fly solo, and look before you leap.

## CHAPTER 3

# Develop a Common Understanding and Intent

Alone we can do so little; together we can do so much.

—(attributed) Helen Keller

Problem solving would be easy to do if leaders could handpick the people they work with, those people of common mind and like spirit, working together to attack problems they all understand. That is not real life. In the education business, highly functional problem-solving teams are few and far between. Members of the varying school communities rarely see their work world in the same way. So, what to do? Enlightened school leaders rarely work with an enlightened faculty team, and on the flip side, few cohesive faculty teams can rely on enlightened leaders. *In reality, to solve problems, leaders and faculties have to learn to work together.*

Dr. Jamie Williams, an All-Pro tight end had just retired. He enrolled in his first semester of doctoral studies. That September, Jamie was taking the author's class in Organization Development. One late afternoon, during a break, Jamie and I struck up a conversation about teamwork. Pro football is a complex game, played at a lightning pace by extraordinary athletes. Perhaps pro ballplayers have the clue for how groups become cohesive teams? So, when asked about how a football squad becomes a team, here is how I remember Jamie responding:

> The game of football is violent. Doing things wrong can get you hurt, or even killed. When playing in the NFL, teamwork is a necessity. When we're on the field, we have to operate as one. We become a team because we have to. It doesn't mean we have to go out to dinner with each other after the game.

Here's the take-away. Most school leaders and faculty members at meetings are probably not with their favorite dinner companions. So to get work done, to solve problems, all those involved have to learn to become one team. When coming together in a workgroup, every member has to learn to operate as one. This means leaders and faculties need to learn how to work together, to come to a common understanding about the problem. It doesn't mean they have to go out to dinner after the meeting is over.

## Getting on the Same Page

Remember, school problems are human problems, and human beings must solve them. Working together to build a common understanding and intent are the fundamental behaviors that make any group successful. This mindset is not automatic. Workgroups disposed to cooperation and consensus do not emerge on their own. Many faculties are fractured and disparate, and their cultures reinforce these negative behaviors. Some even become toxic, battling their way through problem solving, practically guaranteeing a solution will never be found and, if it is stumbled upon, can never be sustained.

The ways to work together and the ways to treat each other are the first conversations and agreements workgroups must form before moving to the work of solving any problem.

Some may think group cohesion is much ado about nothing, a waste of time. Group cooperation is not a big deal. School people have been problem solving for generations. This thinking is a big mistake. Leaders who disregard or give short shrift to the idea of a group needing to develop common understanding and intent are courting disaster.

This chapter addresses the absolutely essential prerequisite before any problem-solving process can be undertaken further, the need for a group to develop common understanding and intent.

## Foibles and Fumbles While Developing a Common Understanding and Intent

Errors and omissions at this stage are ubiquitous. If there is any place in the problem-solving process where school people make mistakes, it's here. Covering all the typical error and omission scenarios here would take the rest of the chapter. Here are four of the more nefarious ones.

## All the World's a Stage

This discussion would be seriously deficient without mentioning those who act out in meetings. Not there to listen, understand, or seek common agreement, these individuals are present to express themselves. Thespians all. This cast of characters is well known: the "know it all," the "orator," the "woe is I," "hog the mic," and the "self-appointed spokesman." If left to their personal scripts, they kidnap agendas while putting on quite a show.

As if on cue, one of these troupers raises a hand, and when recognized, the curtain rises, and the show begins. Lectures, monologues, impassioned pleas, harangues, and tirades parade out one after another, numbing and stupefying the captured audience in attendance. The published agenda, now in shreds, is replaced by a collision of extemporaneous exchanges that leave the purpose of the meeting woefully lost and a beleaguered faculty fast losing its will to live. The product of this theater is the loss of the meeting's purpose, negative meeting outcomes, and frustrated participants. This hostage taking of an agenda is all too common and so very preventable.

## The Food Fight—When the Fringes Are in Control

When problem-solving is allowed to be controlled by the few, the cabals and the saboteurs take over. For them, collaborating to solve problems isn't any fun. They would rather orchestrate mayhem by exploiting those in attendance with indignant rhetoric, bouts of jousting, debate, and pillory. Coming together to solve problems becomes an opportunity to cast blame with impunity, complain with righteous indignation, and pretty much throw a wrench in the entire proceeding. The aim is to start a food fight, and where they are successful, the chance of building group cohesion, collaboration, and commitment dies. Food fights may be fun for this egocentric few, but after the bedlam is over, someone has to clean up the mess. In this scenario, problems are used as cudgels. Meanwhile, problems and their solutions languish backstage at this pointless circus.

## Us Versus Them

You can't trust them. They don't have the real interest of the students at heart. These attributions are used by leaders and faculty alike when describing "the other side." For them, collaborating on a problem means hard-nosed negotiations to result in the most beneficial solution for one side. As to their quality, Margaret Wheatley said it best, "Too many problem-solving sessions become battlegrounds where decisions are made based on power rather than intelligence." When the solution is reached, each party sees its own side. The flip side is seldom understood or cared about by either group. A common understanding and intent are rarely, if ever, gained, and the problem as understood is always filtered through the emotions of the "we" and "they."

## Get On With It

Meetings like this are a waste of my time. School problems are supposed to be solved by the administrators. Attending a problem-solving meeting is actually a form of adult detention. While these individuals make it clear they do not want a part in addressing the problem, they are among the first to criticize a solution that doesn't meet their needs. They adhere to the "show me a rock; no, wrong rock" problem-solving process. They expect others to do the problem-solving work and present them with solutions perfectly matching their criteria. When that doesn't happen, they indignantly demand a new solution be sought.

Unfortunately, this is all too often the reality of how school faculties come to gather to solve school problems. The more unsettling reality is faculty groups and stakeholder groups are made up of representatives from each of the previous scenarios. Members of the *Food Fighters, the Let's Get On With It, the Us Versus Them*, make up a number of the adult population. How important is it to first develop a common understanding and intent on the part of the stakeholders before a productive rational problem-solving process can be entertained? Given the previous discussion, essential.

## Putting It All Together: Develop a Common Understanding and Intent

To operate as one is not easily achieved, let alone a given. As demonstrated by the previous scenarios, not taking the time to develop the group into a functional working unit can have disastrous consequences. Attaining this functionality can be accomplished in three steps, as shown in Figure 3.1. They are the following: Determine the stakeholders, gain

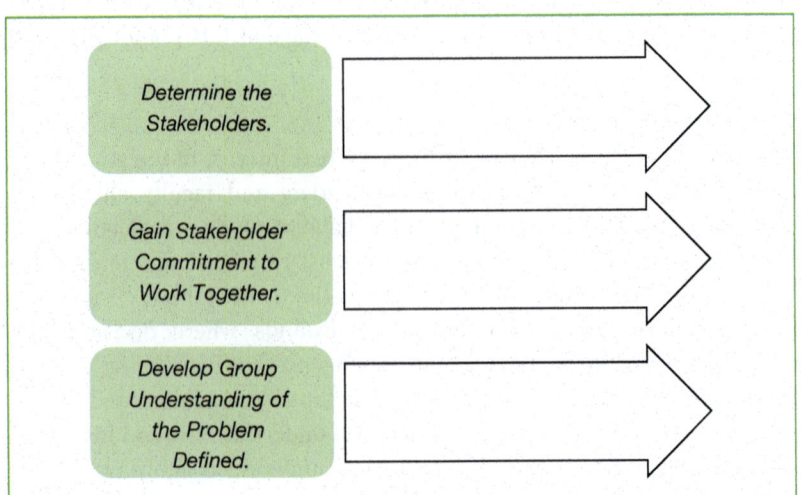

**Figure 3.1** Develop a Common Understanding and Intent

- Determine the Stakeholders.
- Gain Stakeholder Commitment to Work Together.
- Develop Group Understanding of the Problem Defined.

stakeholder commitment, and work to develop a common understanding of the problem as defined.

Determining the stakeholders means identifying the right people to be the problem solvers. Stakeholders have much to win when the problem is solved and much to lose if it isn't. Finding stakeholders begins by determining the origin of the problem. Once pinpointed, stakeholders can be identified, and stakeholder representatives can be selected as part of any problem-solving workgroup. When the stakeholder roster is complete, the problem-solving workgroup has been formed. To start, this is unlikely to include everybody on campus.

This is done by developing guidelines and guide rails that define the normative behavior (norms) dictating how members will treat each other, work together, and meet together. Affirming these norms, the problem-solving workgroup takes on the task of developing the group's common understanding of the problem: its situation, problem type, difficulty, and its urgency to find a solution. The following provides a detailed description for each of these steps.

## Task 1: Determine the Stakeholders

Arguably, when it comes to schools, everyone from the learner to the nation is a stakeholder. For this discussion, a *stakeholder* is defined as an individual who is directly affected by or who can affect a solution to an issue or situation. Why should these people be included?

Here are two examples to demonstrate the importance of stakeholders.

- A state legislature has passed a law stating no child can enroll in a public school without being fully vaccinated against COVID-19. *This is probably a fairly thorny problem.* By definition, a very important stakeholder group would be the parents of the children needing to be enrolled. Consequently, a wise strategy would be to enlist parent representatives to be part of the problem-solving team charged to develop local policy. History provides numerous examples chronicling the chaos and bedlam that ensues when parents are shunned or excluded from participation in this type of situation.

- The college dean has to revise the course curriculum. The faculty responsible for this curriculum are stakeholders. The students taking these courses are stakeholders as well. What would happen if the dean, for whatever reason, solely took on this task, disregarding the constituents?

When stakeholders are not involved in solving the problem, they become part of the problem rather than partners in the search for the solution. Inclusion tends to lead to much happier endings than would result from exclusion.

Stakeholders are found where problems occur and where the effects of problems are felt—the origin of the problem. So how do we pinpoint a problem's origin? Be it an elementary school or a university, schools are subdivided into units while being subparts of a larger social universe. Figure 3.2 depicts the most common way to see this universe. The model depicts each social unit as a concentric circle. Light-colored circles—individual, workgroup institution, and organization—represent the internal makeup of the institution—the school. The dark-colored circles show the local community, state, and nation and represent the constituencies that make up the school's external environment. Problems and their stakeholders can be found in one or more of these circles. Identifying the problem's origin pinpoints the specifics of the situation, the context for deciphering a resolution, and the whereabouts of the stakeholders who can help resolve the problem.

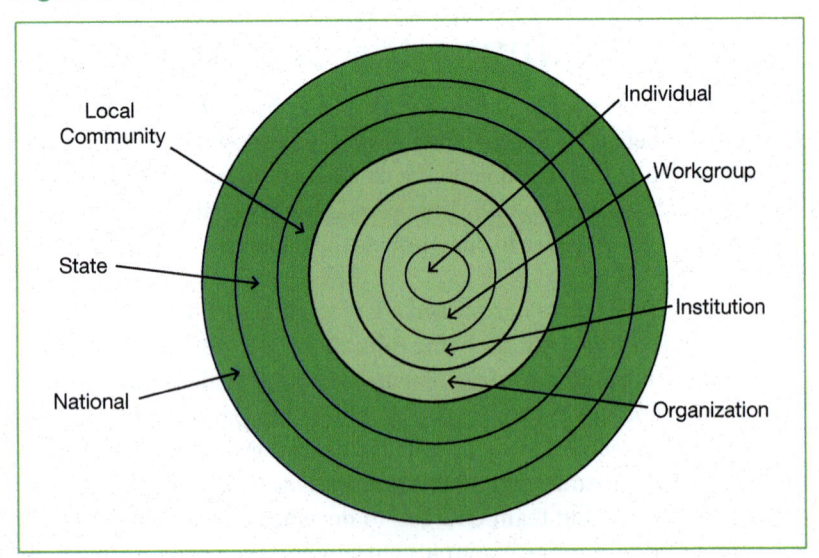

**Figure 3.2** The Social Universe of Schools

*Task. Determine the Origin of the Problem.*
Identify the origin of the problem by using Figure 3.2. Use the problem definition developed from Step 1 as the basis for this inquiry. Once the origin has been pinpointed, work to understand the context and human interaction surrounding the issue. Paint the whole picture, as much as possible.

## TASK CUE CARD

- *Desired Outcome:* The problem's origin and its context have been properly defined.

- *Group Organizers:* The *Thumbs-Up Process* and *Brainstorming*.

- *Your Team Lesson Plan:* Begin by placing a copy of Figure 3.2 on the flipchart or on a whiteboard. Using this illustration, hold a brief discussion with the planning group to pinpoint the origin of the problem. When sufficiently discussed, gain the group's agreement as to the origin using a thumbs up process. Once the agreement has been obtained, have the group determine the breadth and scope of the problem based on its context. Record the comments on the chart board as they are provided. The estimated time for this activity is 10–15 minutes.

*Task. Identify the Problem's Stakeholders.*

**Figure 3.3** The Problem's Stakeholders

|  | Decider | Advisor | Participant |
|---|---|---|---|
| Immediate |  |  |  |
| Proximate |  |  |  |

Remember, stakeholder buy-in is critical to the success of a solution. Completing this task identifies the immediate and peripheral stakeholders, those essential to the process, and those needing to be informed.

## Theoretical Connections

The theoretical foundation for this section is found in Paul Nutt's text *Making Tough Decisions* (1990). Sandy Pokras's text *Team Problem Solving* (1995) covers the stakeholder ideas succinctly. It also provides a practical application of the ideas of this book.

> ### TASK CUE CARD
>
> - *Desired Outcome:* The intermediate and proximate stakeholders are defined. The stakeholder roles in the problem-solving process are determined.
>
> - *Group Organizers: Dyads and Triads* and *Combining and Winnowing*.
>
> - *Your Team Lesson Plan:* Place Figure 3.3 on the flipchart. Begin by explaining the chart elements and explaining the importance of identifying stakeholders and their proximity to the problem. Next, organize members into subgroups of two or three. Have each subgroup define the problem's stakeholders, noting whether they are immediate or proximate. When the subgroups have completed their work, have them report out to the whole group, recording their responses on the Problem Stakeholders chart. Once all information is recorded, work with the entire group to develop a common understanding that identifies the stakeholders. Record that outcome.

## Task 2: Get Stakeholders' Commitment to Work Together

Wow, this is important. When confronting a problem, group cooperation and cohesion are not automatic. In fact, members of school workgroups have many reasons to be disposed otherwise: emotional attachment, personal involvement, cultural orthodoxy, and political allegiances, to name a few. These powerful forces can easily push the group to react in a less than rational manner. Group members must choose to be disposed to a rational course of action devoid of bias, group splintering, and forgone conclusions. Additionally, the group members' frames of mind, or what we call mindset, must be such that each sees the importance of the problem and is fully prepared to honestly participate in finding its solution. Finally, group members must actively work at being team members. Without the right group disposition and mindset, a rational problem-solving process is doomed to failure from the start.

### Look Before You Leap

> ▶ **Rule 4.** Neutralize or eliminate toxic problems before beginning group problem solving.

A fractionated or toxic workgroup will not solve problems well. Even when the splintered group reaches a solution, the solution will be of poor quality and usually unsustainable. When leadership is faced with a fractionated or toxic group, remediating measures must be taken to reshape it. Before moving the group into a problem-solving mode, leadership must go elephant hunting, confront clicks and cabals, surface personal vendettas and squabbles, eliminate cultural blocks, and break territorial silos.

- *Elephant hunting.* Determine if there are elephants in the room—those undiscussable issues and situations that confront the group and prevent it from being cohesive and collaborative. Once the undiscussables are found, bring them out in the open and skillfully have the group deal with them.

- *Confront clicks and cabals.* Splintered groups create splintered solutions. Leadership must confront each click and cabal and gain their commitments to be cooperative and collaborative.

- *Surface personal vendettas and squabbles.* Away from the view of others, leaders bring the combatants together to discuss their grievances and either resolve the conflicts or put them in abeyance while working on the problem.

- *Eliminate cultural blocks.* Working from the superordinate goal, a successful and sustainable solution, leadership must facilitate the building of the intercultural interpersonal bridges necessary to ensure a common understanding of the issues and an equal voice and choice for all parties.

- *Break territorial silos.* Identify departmental or issue-oriented silos. Approaching each silo individually, gain commitments from their membership to be cooperative, collaborative, and open to the ideas and contributions of others.

> **Theoretical Connections**
>
> James Adam's text *Conceptual Blockbusting* (2019) is the seminal read on this topic. Sam Kaner also provides a concise discussion in his text *Facilitator's Guide to Participatory Decision-Making* (2014).

And if these remediations don't work, what next? If time permits, delay the problem-solving sessions until the "deck chairs" can be rearranged and repaired. However, as in most cases, delaying the problem-solving process is not possible. Therefore, the only alternative left is *Option Seven*. How this alternative got its name is unclear, but here it is. When remediated measures fail with either the individuals, or groups above, leadership must either neutralize or eliminate these roadblocks before proceeding. Neutralizing the roadblock means the individual or group, while not willing to cooperate or collaborate, will guarantee to remain neutral and not sabotage or subvert the group process or decision.

If this agreement can't be reached, then the last alternative is to eliminate the individual or group from the process altogether. In this case, working with those who are willing and eliminating the unwilling is a better choice than letting the fox roam freely in the henhouse. Developing an immature group into a cooperative team takes much work, time, and expert mentorship. As discussed in the first chapter, group cohesion and maturity are prerequisites for functional teamwork. These group behaviors should be developed on an ongoing basis and be an important element of the school calendar and not just be considered when problems arise. A number of crucial texts are included in Further Reading.

Here is the big thing to learn about group membership in a problem-solving workgroup. There is only one real requirement for group membership.

> ***Rule 5.*** *The only requirement for membership in a problem-solving workgroup is the individual's disposition to constructively and collaboratively work with others; the rest can be taught.*

### Theoretical Connections

The theoretical texts dealing with toxic groups are many in number. Here are a few of the more important texts on the subject: Dan Levi's book *Group Dynamics for Teams* (2001); *The Wisdom of Teams* (1994), by Katzenbach and Smith; and John Goldhammer's 1996 text *Under the Influence* provide sound foundational knowledge on the subject. Schwarz's *The Skilled Facilitator* (2002) and Weaver and Farrell's 1999 text *Managers as Facilitators* provide are great resources for learning the strategies and tactics for dealing with group dysfunction. The Schwarz, Levi, and Weaver and Farrell texts also provide a clear foundation for the norming process.

## It's About the Norm

It's all said in the Cub Scout "Law of the Pack": *The Cub Scout follows Akela. The Cub Scout helps the pack go. The pack helps the Cub Scout grow. The Cub Scout gives goodwill.*

Phil Jackson put it another way: "The strength of the team is each individual member. The strength of each member is the team." In the United States, getting individuals to work together is a matter of individual choice. As in any relationship where two or more of us come together, the choice requires continued commitment and constant work. For Cub Scouts and NBA ballplayers, each commits to being a team member, and the teams commit to supporting each individual. These commitments are established early on and are constantly practiced.

In essence Cub Scouts and NBA players agree about how they are going to behave. The first order of business for any group is to commit to a certain way of acting when together. They commit to a certain normative behavior. Normative behavior, by definition, is the behaviors, actions, beliefs, and values that are agreed upon as being correct and acceptable by the group participants. This behavior is codified as norms: the ground rules for the group. The codification could be as simple as a list or as sophisticated as a covenant. Regardless of how they are formed, norms are declarative commitments for how each member is to behave, how members treat each other, and how meetings are conducted.

When constructing ground rules, focus on the behaviors the group needs to exhibit to be successful and productive. These would include how individuals are to be treated, how the group will converse, and how differences in opinion or perspective will be ameliorated. They include rules for how conflicts will be managed and resolved. How decisions will be made is also codified. Figure 3.4 depicts the three categories of behavior for norm formulation.

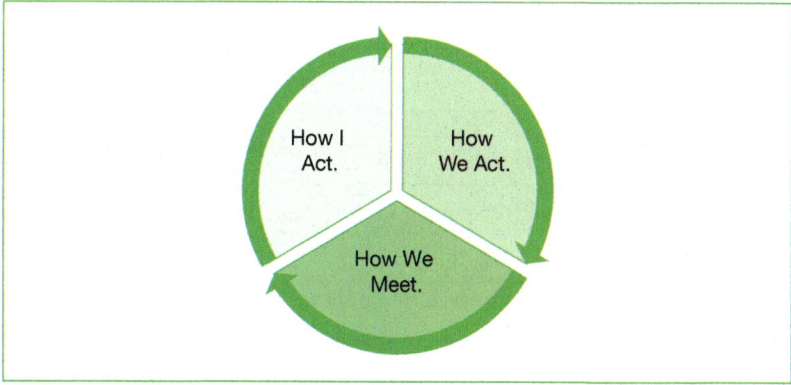

**Figure 3.4** The Three Hows

## How I Act

Each member provides a unique intellectual perspective and vantage point. Members are obligated to themselves and to the group to "speak their truth." Whether it be a value, a belief, or an opinion, the member has the right and obligation to hold it. Additionally, as the British would say, "Each individual has to learn to stand on his or her own legs." Members speak for themselves, speaking their truth clearly without hedging or any "beating around the bush."

Members also need to be responsible and provide the reasons for their position. Each member must be able to differentiate between their declarative statements of knowledge and individual opinion and preference. When expressing what one knows, the member should provide the evidence for that knowledge. When expressing an opinion, he or she should provide the reasoning for the opinion. When engaging in the group conversation, members must question their assumptions, seeking a rational explanation for what is assumed. Before reacting defensively or in opposition to something not understood, members should seek further clarification and definition of the idea or issue proffered, while suspending judgments and checking personal bias. Regardless of how an individual may assess a statement or position taken by another, that position should not be discounted or demeaned. The maxim "treat others as you wish to be treated" should be the guiding behavior.

Finally, all members should agree to reflect. Members should evaluate their behavior and contributions, using three questions. What did I do? How did it work? What do I do next? These questions will show up again in future chapters. Constructive changes of behavior are based on honest reflective thought. As the group reflects to develop and improve the meeting experience, so should each member reflect on improving individual meeting performance. Figure 3.5 lists the more critical behaviors to be considered when building ground rules for *How I Act*.

**Figure 3.5** Essential Elements of Productive Individual Behavior in Groups

| | |
|---|---|
| | Think and speak for myself. |
| | Speak my truth. |
| | Say what I mean. |
| As a member of this group, I will: | State what I know; offer my opinion; know the difference between the two. |
| | Voice my choice. |
| | Keep an open mind, and question my assumptions. |
| | Not act or react to something I do not understand. |
| | Not discount or put down others. |
| | Reflect and adjust. |
| | Not hesitate to admit a mistake, or apologize for a misstep. |

## How We Act

Consider group norms as the vows members take about how they will meet and work together. Figure 3.6 lists a few of the more important ones. Groups first commit to making sure every participant has a seat at the table. Bullies, messiahs, and cabals are not allowed.

Every group has its gregarious few who tend to dominate meetings. However, many important contributions are provided by those who reflect quietly before speaking. When the extroverted members of the group are off to the races, these individuals seldom find the space to express their thoughts. Also, other members won't express their ideas for fear of a negative group reaction. It is the responsibility of the entire group to provide a safe haven for all of its members, a caring environment allowing "airtime" for all. This is a fundamental behavioral requirement.

Meeting groups are far more successful at developing agreements and making decisions when all members focus on their interests rather than taking positions. Positions tend to be concrete and intractable. Holding fast on a position often leads to win and lose scenarios. Intentions, on the other hand, are more malleable. They usually express preferred outcomes and as such, have a much better chance of being integrated into an acceptable outcome for the entire group. When groups work from intentionality, win-win solutions are more likely. Members focus on intention and not position. They work from preferences rather than absolutes.

Collaboration and cooperation fuel high productivity, positive group interaction, and higher levels of member satisfaction. They are indispensable elements of any group's ground rules. When members are more able to trust and respect each other, the group becomes more cohesive. Having a ground rule stating we all will work toward trusting and respecting each other sets an intention. By cooperating and collaborating, that intention can turn into a reality.

Finally, the development and maintenance of quality group behavior is not possible without group metacognition. The importance of each member reflecting on her or his behavior has been previously discussed. It is equally important for the group to do a similar reflection. Without formally addressing the questions What did we do? How did it work? What do we do next? The group has little possibility of changing unproductive group behavior and evolving. While this activity may or may not be part of the meeting agenda, it should be codified in the group's ground rules as a pledge to carry out group self-evaluation with all seriousness.

The previous discussion has identified some of the common individual and group behaviors codified by work groups as guidelines or guardrails for successful meeting experiences. Each meeting group is unique. The ground rules they adopt should be a product of their environment and personality. However, it is suggested that the list provided in Figure 3.6 be used as starting point for the discussion.

**Figure 3.6** Essential Elements of Productive Group Behavior

| | |
|---|---|
| | Allow everyone a seat at the table. |
| | Create a safe space and supportive environment. |
| | Adhere to and support the "ground rules." |
| | Focus on interests not positions. |
| *As a group, we will:* | Encourage the diversity of reasoned thought and opinion. |
| | Work to achieve consensus. |
| | Discuss the undiscussables. |
| | Work to develop team through cooperation and collaboration. |
| | Work to develop mutual trust and respect. |
| | Reflect. |

## How We Meet

Meeting participation is perhaps the most important contributor to meeting success. It begins by members being fully prepared, on time, and being present. Each participant should have reviewed all preparatory materials relating to the agenda and have a clear understanding of what is expected. Being present means any distraction—physical, emotional, and so forth—needs to be put aside. Members should understand their role in contributing to the purpose and output of the meeting. They should also be prepared to seek clarification, where ambiguity occurs, and to suggest additions or amendments to the agenda as they deem appropriate.

Participants should work to maintain a positive attitude and actively work to contribute ideas. Where issues and concerns arise, meeting members should not hesitate to voice them to the group. All participants should practice active listening, suspending judgment, and seeking clarification or definition about issues or ideas that are unclear. They should listen as allies to the ideas of others. When opposing ideas are proffered, members should avoid being defensive and seek to understand the reasoning behind what is being suggested. Finally, members must make commitments to ideas and actions, when required.

When speaking, participants should work at being brief and concise, always being conscious of the unwritten rule of, "sharing airtime." Each member should work hard to avoid interrupting or cutting off another person's conversation. Side conversations and commentary should be avoided completely. The following lists the most egregious participant behaviors and are to be avoided at all costs:

- No griping. Find ways to express discontents as positive corrective actions.
- No bird walks. Stay on point. Be clear and concise.
- Even worse, no "flock flies." Don't bird walk and take others with you.
- No war stories.
- No alpha behavior, which should be left to TV wrestling. Group members engaged in such behavior are at best mildly interesting and, in most cases, unproductive.
- No road hogs. We all love the "mic." Some of us even like to hear ourselves talk. "Airtime" needs to be shared. Be courteous to others. Minimize your speaking time.
- No "Oracles of Delphi." Keep your sage wisdom to yourself.
- No mouthpieces. Don't speak for others.
- No board walking. Don't move from one position to another. Don't waffle. Say what you mean and mean what you say.
- No desert caravans. Don't lead or be a part of wandering inanely from topic to topic.
- No gab fests. Keep side conversations for after the meeting.

Figure 3.7 lists the more important norms to be followed when groups meet.

**Figure 3.7** Essential Elements of Productive Meeting Behavior

| | |
|---|---|
| | Be on time and be present. |
| | Maintain a positive attitude and work actively to contribute. |
| | Actively listen. |
| *When we meet, we will:* | Suspend judgment. |
| | Seek clarification and definition about issues and ideas that unclear. |
| | Make commitments when required. |
| | Share airtime. Be brief and concise when speaking. |
| | Avoid interrupting or cutting off another member's comments. |
| | Not engage in side conversations or side comments. |

*Task. Gain Stakeholder Commitment to Work Together.*
Here is the big thing to learn about working with newly formed groups: "In order to go fast, you have to go slow." It's always process before task. The group needs to figure out how to behave, how to treat each other, and how to meet before it can solve problems.

> **Rule 6.** *The group must be organized and agree to its norms and meeting rules before addressing the task of problem solving.*

## TASK CUE CARD

- *Desired Outcome:* The stakeholder group organizes and develops the normative behaviors for personal deportment, group interaction, and meeting etiquette.

- *Group Organizers: Snow Cards, Gallery Walk, Combining and Winnowing, Consensus. (See the glossary for complete directions for doing Snow Cards and the Gallery Walk.)*

- *Your Team Lesson Plan:* Place Figures 3.4–3.7 on four flipcharts. Begin by explaining "The Three Hows," and why group agreement to norms is so important to group success. Using Figures 3.5–3.7, discuss each chart's contents. Ensure member understanding by clarifying and defining.

- Next, explain snow carding. Distribute an ample number of 3 by 5 cards or sticky notes to each member. Have members write down the norms they wish to see the group adopt—one per sheet/card. Make sure members address all three charts.

- When the group has completed its work, have each of the members post their cards or sticky notes on the corresponding chart—that is, "How I Act" cards, the blank "How I Act" chart, and so forth.

- Once all information is recorded, have the members do a Gallery Walk to study the norms posted. Allow sufficient time for the group to process. After completing the Walk conduct a Combining and Winnowing exercise and pair down the norm lists to their final editions.

- Conduct a consensus process for each set of norms. Ensure all members either agree or will go along with each norm. Celebrate and have the group applaud their work—the group has just completed its first problem-solving exercise.

- The estimated time for this activity is 2–3 hours in either 1 or 2 sessions.

# Task 3: Develop Understanding of the Problem Defined

Wasn't this done before? The answer is yes. The planning group developed a written-problem statement describing the elements, type, difficulty, and urgency of the situation to be addressed. The easy thing to do here is to post a written problem statement as a given and proceed into the problem-solving process. Here's the rub. This is a new group. Members have one thing in common; they are problem stakeholders. Each has a personal reason to solve the problem and a particular perception and vantage point from which to solve it. These individual positions are not yet in alignment.

> **Theoretical Connections**
>
> The theoretical foundation for this section is found in Paul Nutt's 1990 text, *Making Tough Decisions*. Sandy Pokras's 1995 text *Team Problem Solving* covers the stakeholder ideas succinctly. It also provides a practical discussion of the ideas of this book.

Also, some members of the stakeholder team were part of the formulation of the written problem statement and have ownership of it. The newly added members have not had the opportunity to "voice and choice" their rendition of the problem, and most likely have new ways of defining the situation in question. Failure to allow these groups the opportunity to develop the problem definition in common will splinter the group and create the "insiders" group and the "newbies." That's a bad idea. Rather than falling into that rabbit hole and creating a fractionated group for the sake of expediency, take time here to develop the group's common understanding and mindset of the problem to insure group cohesion. Get the group on the same page, and create a common mindset. This is the starting point for creating the problem's solution.

*Task. Stakeholder Group Develops a Common Mindset and Definition of the Problem.*
While the outcome for this task is the common definition of the problem by the stakeholder group, pay attention to two other important issues. First, work hard at applying the meeting norms and procedures agreed to by the group. Second, attend to the development of cohesion. It is important for leadership to not only facilitate completion of the task but also to manage the meeting according to previous agreements. Support positive group development. Begin by affirming to the group that some members have invested much time in defining the problem and producing the written problem statement. Acknowledge their contribution and ownership. Then, welcome

and acknowledge the importance of new members and the fresh perspectives they bring to the problem-solving table. Finally, congratulate the entire group on the previous work they've done with group norms. Have the group membership reflect on the norms and meeting procedures they have agreed to, and proceed to the session task.

### TASK CUE CARD

- *Desired Outcome:* The stakeholder group develops a common description and definition of the problem.

- *Group Organizers: The Clarification Process and Consensus Process*

- *Your Team Lesson Plan:* As part of pre-meeting preparation, send the meeting agenda and the written problem statement along with appropriate background material to each stakeholder member. Instruct them to study the material and be prepared to discuss it.

- Begin the meeting by acknowledging group membership (referred to opening comments above). Post a written problem statement on a flipchart. Have members of the planning team present the statement to the group. Provide the group time to ask questions for clarification. Once completed, ask for amendments to the statement. Incorporate accepted amendments, and finalize the statement. Finally, conduct a consensus process to ensure that each member agrees to how the statement is written and is willing to act on it. The estimated time to complete this task is 1–2 hours.

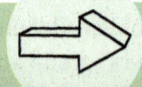

### Consider This . . .

Forming in-house teams can't happen soon enough. No, this is not a suggestion for adding hours of extra meetings to any staff member's life. It is a reminder that there will always be problems that need solving. It's as certain as death and taxes. A good leader will know not only what is going on in the school or in school units but also which staff members can be counted on to be solid members of any team. A good leader knows the local community as well and keeps in touch with those who have served well as problem solvers as well as newcomers who might be called on to help with an immediate problem or issue. You only have to start from scratch once to be well prepared for the problem that will no doubt arrive on the first day of school every year.

Identify and Define the Problem. → Develop a Common Understanding and Intent. → **Image the Solution and Determine Its Impact.** (You are here.) → Develop Solution Criteria and Select Problem-Solving Procedure. → Define Search Strategies and Find Solution Alternatives. → Weigh Alternatives and Decide on a Solution. → Solve the Problem.

CHAPTER 4

# Image the Solution and Determine Its Impact

There's no use talking about the problem unless you talk about the solution.

—Betty Williams

Visualize your success; then act.

—Anonymous

"Where does it make berth?"

Have you not heard this story? Captain Barbosa and his crew of miscreants sail from the dreaded Isla de la Muerta.

"It's an island that cannot be found except by those who already know where it is," confides Captain Jack Sparrow to Will Turner.

Solutions to problems are like that island from a movie. Solutions to problems are not easily found unless there is a sense of what their solution looks like.

The group is now armed with a comprehensive understanding of the problem having developed an inclusive and accurate statement that defines and describes the problem. What next? Going helter-skelter in search of a solution at this point will result in much flailing about. The group needs to a have idea of what it is looking for. The next step is to theorize a resolution of the problem by visualizing what it should look like and determining the way to get there. This is not a foreign idea; we all create mental models of the desired conditions to fix the problems. All humans visualize solutions as they rationally problem solve. Here is a simple example to illustrate this idea.

A person is walking down the street trying to reach a destination two blocks away. When reaching a street corner, the signal light at the crosswalk is flashing red; the thoroughfare is uncrossable. Correctly assessing the situation, this person stops at the curb and waits. The flashing light turns green, and the opposing traffic is now stopped at the intersection. It's now safe to proceed. The question is, how does this person know when to stop and when it's safe to cross? The answer is simple. The person has visualized that when the light is red, traffic is proceeding through the intersection, and it is unsafe to cross. When the light turns green and the cross traffic stops; it's now safe to cross. The problem of crossing the street is solved by associating a prior understanding with the present situation to know how to solve it. Think about it. When children are first taught to navigate a city's streets, someone teaches them how to associate using the "if this, then this" logic to solve this street-crossing problem. The child is taught to solve the problem by imaging the solution: stop, when red; go, when green. So the desired state of reaching the other side of the street is accomplished by understanding the process of red light, green light.

Seeing a picture of the problem solved allows for a comparison with the problem situation. Noticing the gap between the two uncovers the map to the solution. The problem is known; a solution is envisioned; the path to a viable solution can now be charted.

The group has defined the problem. The next logical step is to determine what ought to be. This is the process of imaging a solution. Before going forward, let's define the idea of a solution.

The word *solution* has two definitions. A solution is both the outcome and the process.

- As the outcome, a solution is the state or fact of a problem being solved. The resolution of the problem.

- As a process, a solution is the means by which a problem can be solved. The appropriate process for reaching the correct outcome.

When the group images a solution to a problem, they must first imagine the outcome, the desired end state, and then determine the process for how to get there. This chapter addresses the first element, how a group constructs or creates a picture of the outcome, what the situation would look like if the problem were solved. Using the definitions and descriptions of the problem, the group visualizes and describes the whos, whats, wheres, whens, and whys of the resolved situation, the desired end state. Once that picture has been painted, it is then overlaid on the entire organization to see what unintended changes were created. The unintended consequences paired with the picture of the desired end state form the image of what the solution should look like. This mental model becomes the template for what to look for when seeking a solution. The second element of imaging a solution is mapping the process for finding the solution. This task is covered in the next chapter.

## Foibles and Fumbles While Imaging a Solution and Selecting a Problem-Solving Procedure

Only the more skilled workgroups have learned to take the time to start with an end state in mind. What happens when the workgroup neglects to image a solution? Well, "You're off the edge of the map here, mate." "Here be monsters." Let's take a peek at situations to avoid.

### The Seventeens

These are the ready, fire, don't worry about aiming folks. They have no time to bother with the intermediate steps of imaging the solution, developing a problem-solving process, or for that matter, seeking alternatives. These groups identify a problem and start throwing solutions against the wall until something sticks.

The *Seventeens* come in many flavors. The *Too Cool Crowd*; a self-assured, subtly haughty group that always knows best. Problem-solving stuff is a waste of time. Whatever we come up with will be superior to anyone else's answer.

Then there's the *Hit-And-Run Gang*. They simply have no time to seek a rational solution. They identify the problem, triage it, put some bandages on it, and hope it heals itself.

While observing a *Seventeens* group in action, a wise colleague mused: "You know, we never have the time to do it right the first time, but we have the infinite capacity to do it over, and over, and over again." Veteran leaders know, there are no shortcuts; there's no free lunch.

Why are these groups called *Seventeens*? When needing to solve a problem, A Seventeens group dashes from *Step 1*, Identifying the Problem, to *Step 7*, Solving the Problem, without taking time to stop and think.

### The Shoehorners

It's the hammer, and the everything's a nail mess arrives again. These groups already have an all-purpose solution in mind. It may be the "tried and true" "break the glass in case of fire" option. Perhaps it's the "CYA option." Maybe if no one is looking, "the thing they always wanted to sneak in" solution. A problem identified presents the opportunity to wedge and hammer a favored predetermined solution into place. Just shoehorn it in and make it fit to solve the problem. Another way of looking at this is the *Shoehorner* folks have a solution looking for a problem.

This conversation would not be complete without giving a shout-out to a special category of Shoehorner, *the Conference Crusader*. A disclaimer is appropriate here. Some information leaders learn at conferences is constructive and can lead to important innovations. These ideas address the salient issues confronting the organization and offer possible solutions. These are not the nuggets *Conference Crusaders* bring back. *Conference Crusaders* make their bones by bringing back the latest flavor of the month. Whatever the trend, we're doing it, whether useful or not.

Anyone who has experienced being "shoehorned" knows the problem-solving process either becomes a slick sales job or an orchestrated set of political maneuvers, maybe both. For those bystanders participating in the process, it feels like you're being conned or pressured to go along to get along. Those shoehorned feel no ownership of the choice or its implementation. Sustaining a shoehorned solution is problematic. A shoe that doesn't fit pinches, as does a "shoehorned" solution to a problem.

## The Research Says

Want to impress and speak with authority but don't have the time or inclination to do the ground work necessary? Practice scholastic alchemy. You know, cribbing. Instead, skim the "————————for Dummies" version, or grab a punchline from the current best-selling treatise. Do sloppy science.

Here's the recipe. Get a piece of work by somebody who maybe knows something. Where do you find it? That's easy. Go to Amazon bestsellers, or for extra bonus points, use the book your boss is currently pushing. Here's where the cribbing comes in. Don't use the text as a starting point for a serious scholarly investigation. Just read a chapter or somebody's PowerPoint. Make up a few glib remarks for evidence, and you're armed. Put on your black horn rimmed and head into the meeting. Wait for it. Wait for it. The discussion is focusing on imaging a solution. Now, hit the group with the mic-dropping phrase "the research says" and let er' rip. Confidently lecture the group with gross generalities, using your best professorial voice. You can click your pen for emphasis to get a more dramatic effect. End your lecturette by doing an authoritative clearing of the throat. Look at you; you're smokin'.

You have taken the advice of that old Latin phrase, *vestis virum facit*. It's not what you know, it is how you look that makes a difference. Whether your comments hold water is mildly interesting. You've got that "research" gig down. You are a full-fledged academic alchemist. You can impress with authority those who don't see through your ruse, but there are very few of your colleagues who don't. An alchemist is not a scientist.

## Barnyard Follies Featuring Chicken Little and the Hysterics

Both the emotional and rational intelligences of healthy groups are in balance; both function in a complementary fashion. However, some groups have a singularly rational personality. They are dispassionate, linear thinking folks. Here, the focus is on the hyper-sensitive *Hysterics* led by, you guessed it, *Chicken Little*. The particular personality of the *Hysterics* dictates they must emotionally overreact to problems. When the problem is brought to the floor, the shrill of an emotional response redirects the proceedings. "What's going to happen to me?" is loudly blurted out by a *Chicken Little*, and then the follies begin. The plea spreads like a plague and soon infects the entire gaggle. One *Hysteric* after another outdoes the previous speaker's supplication with a more soulful "woe is I." The meeting descends into a dark chorus of helpless voices. Left unchecked, the proceedings devolve into a testification of nonsensical cackles, leaving common sense in the dust. The wringing of proverbial hands, voices getting louder and louder, creates a sort of self-inflicted version of an institutional PTSD, which is dropped on the group like a wet blanket ending the doleful dance of our headless chickens. Sometimes bad is just bad.

## Putting It All Together: Imaging the Solution and Determining Its Impact

Schools are incredibly busy places. Staffs aren't just sitting around waiting for problems to arise so they can solve them. There are students to see, papers to correct, lessons to plan, parents to contact. The list seems endless. Time is always in short supply. Dealing with problems that are not on one's immediate personal agenda is always an added hassle. Everyone wants to dispense with those intruding problems with great dispatch. There's a problem. Let's just get to the solution.

> ▶ **Rule 7.** *Successful problem solving must begin with an end in mind—a coherent image of the solution and a defined path to get there. There are no shortcuts. Begin at the beginning.*

Take the time to save time. Get it right the first time. Finding the right solution becomes an almost impossible task if there is no sense of what the solution should look like or how the solution can be reached. The group's next task is to picture the resolution of the problem—the desired end state.

**Figure 4.1** Imaging the Solution Outcome

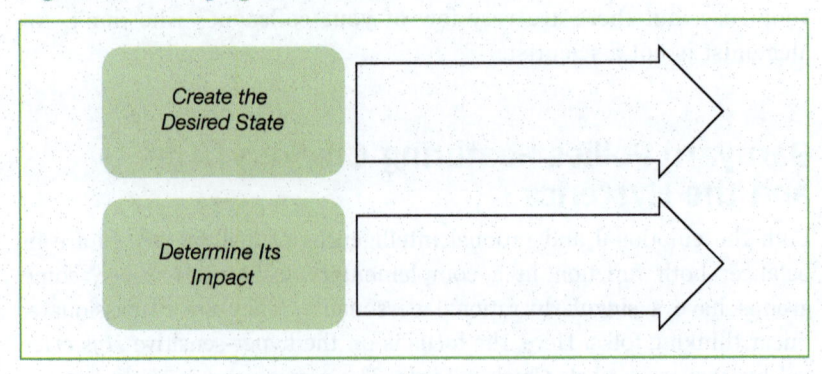

Create the Desired State

Determine Its Impact

As shown is Figure 4.1, creating the solution outcome is accomplished by imaging the desired state and determining what additional effects the solution creates for the rest of the organization. Since most school groups have little experience at imaging a preferred "end state," the resolution of the problem, take the time needed to make sure the group understands the task and is on board with it. The group may feel uncomfortable at first, seeing this task as nebulous and frivolous. Good meeting preparation and preliminary coaching will be extremely helpful here. Here is the formula that creates the problem solution.

## Discrepancy Analysis

A discrepancy analysis, as shown in Figure 4.2, is a metacognitive process that answers three questions. What is? What should be? What's the difference?

**Figure 4.2** Discrepancy Analysis

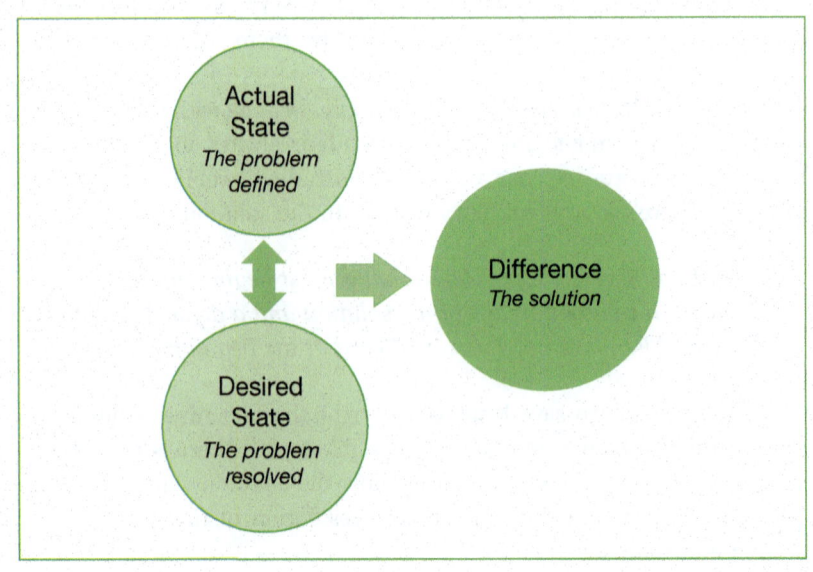

Actual State
*The problem defined*

Desired State
*The problem resolved*

Difference
*The solution*

The discrepancy analysis process examines the differences between the desired solution state and the actual state of the problem identifying where the discrepancy, or gap, exists between the desired and actual state creates the elements of the solution.

Here is how it works:

1. The problem is defined. The situation or outcome is described in detail.

2. The resolution of the problem is theorized or imagined. The desired state is then described in detail.

3. The required solution is determined. The discrepancy or gap between what is and what should be is described to determine what is needed.

The problem-solving group follows this formula when imaging a solution. Using the detailed definition or description of the problem, the group first imagines or theorizes what the resolution of the problem looks like. Next, they compare the problem stated to the imagined problem resolved. Seeing the discrepancies, they define the elements and processes needed to close the gap to create a solution framework, to guide the search for an appropriate solution, and to judge the options found. The remainder of this chapter will describe how the first task is accomplish by the problem-solving group.

## Task 1: Creating the Desired State

How does the group go about imagining the desired state?

Imagination is the process of putting mental images together to tell a story. In order to begin the process, the group suits up by putting themselves into a specific state of mind.

Walt Disney's Imagineers have been creating Disney's future for well over a half century. They image their solutions, and then go about making them happen. They seem to be pretty good at it. Based on the rules of the Imagineers, here are a few things to consider when the group is going to image a solution:

- Know the stakeholders. Be clear about their requirements for a solution.

- Wear your stakeholders' shoes. Experience the solution from their point of view. Don't forget the human factors.

- Organize the flow of the people, the tasks, and the ideas needed in a logical fashion.

- Only image the intended solution, the whole solution, and nothing but the solution.

- Integrate different views and viewpoints.

- Keep at it. Persist at the task until the image is clear.

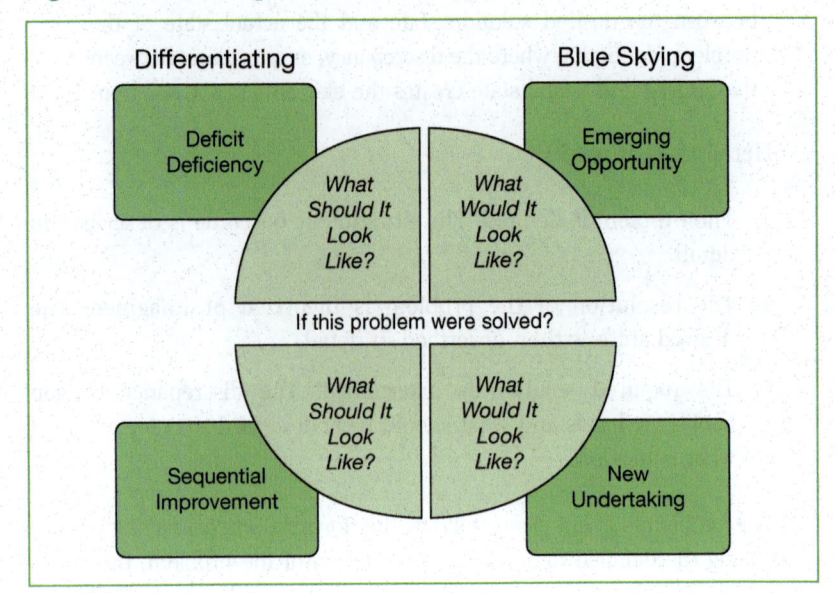

**Figure 4.3** Creating the Solution Image

```
        Differentiating                    Blue Skying

    ┌─────────────┐                            ┌─────────────┐
    │   Deficit   │                            │  Emerging   │
    │ Deficiency  │    What        What        │ Opportunity │
    └─────────────┘   Should It   Would It     └─────────────┘
                      Look        Look
                      Like?       Like?

                   If this problem were solved?

                      What        What
    ┌─────────────┐   Should It   Would It     ┌─────────────┐
    │             │   Look        Look         │             │
    │ Sequential  │   Like?       Like?        │    New      │
    │ Improvement │                            │ Undertaking │
    └─────────────┘                            └─────────────┘
```

## Imaging the Desired State

The process begins by gathering the results of the 5Ws and the identification of the particular problem type to formulate *the actual state*, the starting point for imaging a solution. As shown in Figure 4.3, problem types require different ways to think about imaging the resolution.

Four types of problems were considered in Chapter 2: *deficit or deficiency, sequential improvement, emerging opportunity,* and *new undertaking.*

- Groups react to *deficits, deficiencies, and improvements*. They visualize an image that fixes the problem. They are picturing the scene of *What Should Be,* a solution that reconciles or remediates the problem.

- Groups are proactive when they address *emerging opportunities* and *new undertakings*. Here groups have to vision an image of something yet to be. Not dependent or constrained by past practice, they create the solution from thin air. They *Blue Sky.* They are picturing the *What Would Be or Could Be.*

## Theoretical Connections

A great text explaining creative thinking is Joyce Wycoff's (1995) book *Transformational Thinking.*

Guiding questions are used to focus the group's imagination and to channel their responses. The guiding question for reactive problems centers the visualization on what *should* the solution look like. The guiding question for proactive problems centers the visualization on what *would* the solution look like. The 5Ws supply the characters, action, setting, and plot of the solution image. Who are the people in the solution? What are they doing? Where are they doing it? How long? What are the results? Why does this resolution work? Here are two simple examples taken from Chapter 2 to demonstrate how questioning could be used to guide in the development of a potential solution.

> A *deficit* or *deficiency problem*. *The principal is informed that school expenditures exceeded the budget allocated, thus creating a deficit.*
>
> In this example, the group is reacting to the situation. Having defined the problem as a deficit issue, the group constructs an image of what the situation should be if the budget were in balance by asking the question, If the budget deficit were solved, what should expenditures look like? What should revenues look like? Using the 5Ws, they create a portrait of the preferred solution. They picture the revenue, personnel, instructional materials, supplies, maintenance, and operations activities that are in place when the problem has been solved.
>
> A *sequential improvement problem* is approached in this same way; the problem-solving group envisions a solution for the situation when the improvement has been achieved.
>
> The second scenario is a simple example of a common proactive problem.

> *Emerging opportunity.* *An elementary principal has been notified that grant opportunities are available for reading improvement initiatives.*
>
> Having identified this situation as an opportunity, the problem-solving group creates an image of what the school reading program would look like when the grant was in effect. Again, using the 5Ws, they picture what teachers and students are doing, what other school staff are doing, where the programs are being conducted, what materials and technology are being used, and what methods of instruction are being employed. This portrait is then documented.

The image for a *new venture* problem also employs the *What Would Be* line of reasoning.

## Creative Thinking Requires a Creative Space

Just a word about setting and temperament. Since the creative process requires an intense amount of free thought, providing an accommodating setting is necessary for success. The environment should be inviting, a place where the group can feel free to be open and spontaneous. A creative setting is comfortable and free from distractions, with the tools and resources necessary to support quality thinking. The space provides for the group's human needs and is sequestered from the outside world. The creative workspace is an incubator of sorts.

While locale is an essential ingredient, creative thinking also requires a certain mindset and way of thinking by the group. Members should be predisposed to doing the following:

- Suspending judgment. Let ideas be in the room without prematurely evaluating their worth.

- Checking assumptions. Verify what is believed to be true. Verify facts. Assume nothing.

- Engaging in playful thinking. Engage in thinking that encourages novelty, creativity, and the imagination.

- Keeping an open mind, a willingness to listen to and to look at all ideas.

- Being fearless. Challenge personal mental barriers and self-imposed restraints.

- Above all, be a part of the constructive conversation.

Creative thinking is not a process most groups have experience doing. Appropriate support and assistance by leadership, as well as a thoughtful meeting design and careful use of Group Organizers will go a long way in making these tasks successful.

*Task. Stakeholder Group Develops an Image of the Desired State, the Resolution of the Problem.*
Reactive and proactive meetings have different tenors and stressors, prepare accordingly.

Leadership might need to help lower the group's adrenaline and angst with a *reactive* issue while needing to set a creative atmosphere and stage for the *proactive* problem. Visualizing the meeting proceeding beforehand will be invaluable to meeting planning.

## Theoretical Connections

The theoretical foundations and an expansion of the ideas presented here can be found in the following texts. John Hayes's *The Complete Problem Solver* (1989); Lyles's (1982) text *Practical Management Problem Solving and Decision Making,* and *Thinking and Problem Solving* (1998), Robert Sternberg, editor.

# TASK CUE CARD FOR DEFICIT/ DEFICIENCY, SEQUENTIAL IMPROVEMENT

- *Desired Outcome:* The stakeholder group has developed a comprehensive image of the problem solution.

- *Group Organizers: Nominal Group Technique, Mind Mapping, Combining, Winnowing,* and *Consensus Processes*

- *Your Team Lesson Plan:* Prior to the meeting, distribute the problem statement, 5Ws, and problem-type background material to group members for review. Have the members think about what a solution would look like and how the 5Ws would play out in a potential solution. Ensure that the meeting space meets the criteria as previously defined in this section.

- Place Figures 2.2, 2.3, 4.2, and a readable copy of the problem statement in a prominent position so all group members can easily reference them. Affix a 3 × 8 foot of paper on a side wall, ensuring it is visible to all participants.

- Begin the meeting with a transition exercise—a *Check-In* or a short reflective period. Once completed, review the agenda and explain the type of thinking required to make the meeting successful. Review with members the predispositions discussed earlier. Get member buy-in. Have members review the Figures 2.2, 2.3, and the problem statement posted. Allow time for clarification questions.

- Once a common understanding is present, explain Figure 4.2. Set guiding questions for the exercise, and explain the sub-questions used based on the 5Ws (Figure 2.2). Lead the group through a *Nominal Technique Group Organizer* (see glossary for detailed directions). Ensure that each member has a pen and sticky notes. Explain the rules of the *Group Organizer* to the group. Go to the blank chart on the side wall; place the guiding question in the center, with branches for each of the 5Ws. Pose the guiding question to the group: *If the problem were solved, what should it look like?* Provide appropriate reflective time for members to consider a response.

- After sufficient time has elapsed, have the group members affix their responses by sticky note to the appropriate 5W. Once completed, conduct a conversation about
what was created. Amend the map as appropriate.

- Enlist a team of writers to create a solution statement based on the *Mind Map*. Complete this activity with a group celebration. Adjourn to allow the statement to be created. Reconvene. Use a consensus process from the glossary to gain agreement on the solution image. Estimated time for completion is 1–2 hours for the *Nominal Group Technique*, 15–45 minutes for the consensus process.

# TASK CUE CARD FOR EMERGING OPPORTUNITY OR NEW VENTURE

- *Desired Outcome:* The stakeholder group has developed a comprehensive image of the problem solution.

- *Group Organizers: Mind Scaping, Clarification,* and *Consensus Processes*

- *Your Team Lesson Plan:* Prior to the meeting, distribute the problem statement, 5Ws, and problem-type background material to group members for review. Have the members think about what a solution would look like and how the 5Ws would play out in a potential solution. Ensure the meeting space meets the criteria as previously defined. Place Figures 2.2, 2.3, 4.2, and readable copy of the problem statement in a prominent position where group members have easy reference.

- Affix a 3 × 8 foot of paper on a side wall, ensuring visibility to all participants. Begin the meeting with a transition exercise such as checking in, a quick meditation, or a period of silence. Once completed, review the agenda and explain the type of thinking required to make the meeting successful. Review with members the pre-dispositions discussed earlier. Get member buy-in. Have members review the Figures 2.2, 2.3, and the problem statement posted.

- Allow time for clarification questions. Once a common understanding is present, explain Figure 4.2. Set guiding questions for the exercise, and explain the sub-questions used based on the 5Ws (Figure 2.2). Lead the group through a *Mind Scaping Group Organizer* (see glossary for detailed directions). Ensure that each member has the appropriate supplies.

- Explain the rules of *Mind Scaping* to the group. Place the guiding question in the center of the sidewall of the blank chart. Draw branches for each of the 5Ws. Pose the guiding question to the group: *If the problem were solved, what would it look like?* Provide appropriate reflective time for members to consider a response. After sufficient time has elapsed, have the group members record their responses on the *Mind Map* in a freeform fashion that uses the materials provided. Allow members to expound and expand on each other's work. Ideas can be posted in writing, graphically, or by sketch. At the completion of the activity, conduct a conversation about what was created. Amend the map as appropriate.

- Enlist a team of writers to create a solution statement describing the *Mind Scape.* When concluding, celebrate the accomplishment. Adjourn to allow the statement to be created. Reconvene, and use a consensus process from the glossary to gain agreement on the solution image statement. Estimated time for completion is 1–2 hours for the Mindscape, 15–45 minutes for the consensus process.

# Task 2: Determine the Solution Impact

**Figure 4.4** SWOT the Effects of the Resolution to the Problem

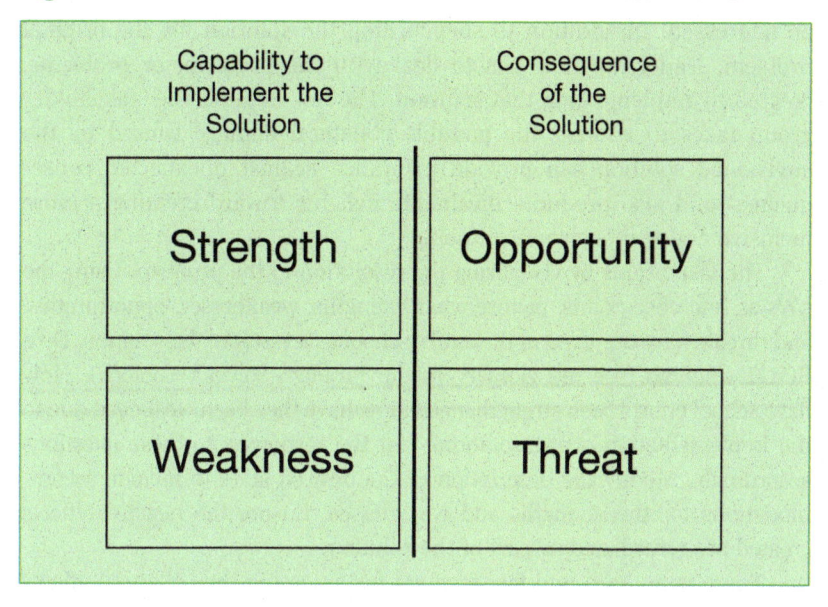

|  Capability to Implement the Solution | Consequence of the Solution |
|---|---|
| Strength | Opportunity |
| Weakness | Threat |

Changes don't happen in a vacuum. When one thing changes in a school, everything else is affected to some degree. When a solution is implemented, there can be unintended effects. Before completing the image of any desired solution, consider its impacts on the rest of the school's operations. Does the resolution advance the school's mission and goals? Is carrying out the resolution worth the effort needed to implement it? How does the resolution tax present resources? What are the effects of the resolution on the present culture? How will the resolution fit with the present school operations? These are a few of the important questions to consider when weighing the impact of implementing a solution to a problem. When creating the resolution to the problem, take the additional fail-safe step to imagine the overall effects the potential solution will have, and factor those issues into the description of the resolution (Figure 4.4).

In most cases, the adjustments uncovered can easily be accommodated. However, if the resolution envisioned creates problems, wouldn't it be a good idea to know that before proceeding? Under certain circumstances, the problems created by the solution may be so disruptive that proceeding to address the issue might not be worth the effort. On the other hand, what problem presented is so grievous that it must be solved regardless of its consequences on the rest of the school? Wouldn't it be smart to consider to how to prepare for the fallout as part the solution?

Some advice given to the authors long ago seems appropriate to recount here.

> ***Rule 8.*** *You don't really solve a problem when by resolving it, you inadvertently create a new one.*

When a solution creates a new problem, now two problems need to be addressed. In addition to shepherding the solution for the original problem, leadership now has to deal with the problem, or problems, created by implementing that solution. The few minutes the stakeholder group takes to address the possible collateral damage caused by the envisioned solution can provide insurance against unexpected consequences and also produces invaluable insights toward creating a more inclusive and responsive resolution.

The task begins by visualizing the resolution to the problem. Using the 5Ws as reference points, picture what strengths, weaknesses, opportunities, and threats have occurred in the entire school as a result of the solution. Do a *SWOT analysis* (see the glossary in the Problem-Solver's Toolbox). How have school efforts been strengthened? How have they been weakened due to the implementation of the solution? List the responses to these questions accordingly. Modify the description of the desired state to include accommodations for the strengths and weaknesses. Ensure the negative effects created are remediated as part of the solution.

There is no hard and fast formula for assessing the collateral effects of a solution on total school operations as situations vary. Each problem should be assessed based on the urgency to solve it and the degree to which the solution provides a positive impact on the school.

*Task. Determine the Collateral Effects as a Result of the Resolution to the Problem.*
Explain to the group that a resolution to a problem can impact the present school situation in many ways, some negatively. Explain how the SWOT will be used to assess solution impact on total school efforts. Finally, point out to the group the outcome for this task is to identify the solution's positive and negative impacts on the school unit and to make the necessary adjustments to the current resolution to the problem accordingly.

## TASK CUE CARD

- *Desired Outcome:* The collateral effects accommodated by the resolution to the problem.

- *Group Organizers: Sticky Notes, Winnowing Process,* and *a T-chart Process* are the Group Organizers used here.

- *Your Team Gameplan:* From flipcharts, present Figure 4.4 to the group. Review the charts with the group. Explain how the solution creates strengths, weaknesses, opportunities, and threats to the existing school situation. Review how a SWOT works.

- Explain the purpose of this task is to uncover those positive and negative effects and make the adjustments necessary to eliminate any negative effects. Check for understanding.

- Now ask the group members to study the newly created resolution statement and its supporting documentation. Provide sufficient time for members to understand the information.

- Have each member identify the strengths, weaknesses, opportunities, and threats to the rest of the school created by the resolution. They are to record each finding on a sticky note.

- As members complete the task, have them post their responses on the appropriate SWOT quadrant on Figure 4.4.

- Have the group examine weaknesses and threats posed by the solution.

- Have the group winnow and combine the responses to create the final list.

- Create a T-chart with the left column titled *Effect* and the right column titled *Accommodation*. Review each weakness and threat and have the group brainstorm the remediation for each. Record the results on the T-chart.

- Once completed, have the writing team add the *accommodation* items to the *resolution to the problem* statement.

- The estimated time to complete this task is 30–45 minutes.

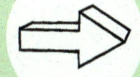

## Consider This . . .

At this point, you and the team may be feeling as though this entire problem-solving method may not work considering the effort it requires. If so, consider the consequences of not solving the problem successfully. How often has a problem solving resulted in the plan lasting until the meeting attendees have left the room and returned to their usual routine? Buy-in is essential and can only happen if the solution found is shared with the stakeholders in a manner that is as rational as the way the solution has been discovered. Take the time to do it all correctly, and save time by not having to do it again . . . and again . . . and again.

You are here.

| Identify and Define the Problem. | Develop a Common Understanding and Intent. | Image the Solution and Determine Its Impact. | **Develop Solution Criteria and Select Problem-Solving Procedure.** | Define Search Strategies and Find Solution Alternatives. | Weigh Alternatives and Decide on a Solution. | Solve the Problem. |

**CHAPTER 5**

# Develop the Solution Criteria and Select a Problem-Solving Procedure

> There were several additions of a later date; but, above all, three crosses of red ink, two on the north part of the island, one in the south-west, and beside this last, in the same red ink, and in a small, neat hand, very different from the captain's tottery characters, these words: 'Bulk of treasure here.'
>
> —*Treasure Island*, Robert Lewis Stevenson (1883)

And as the good Captain Sparrow quipped to Will Turner, "Knowing the location of the island is one thing. Getting there is another." Wouldn't it be nice if the treasure's exact location was known? There are thousands of islands out there. Many look the same.

Searching for treasure without a map is a fool's errand. Even with the map, the search itself can be an adventure. If not properly charted and navigated by an excellent crew, great planning can lead to disaster.

There are some points to be made from this pirate chatter.

Not having a clear map for choosing a solution to a problem is taking the same fool's path as searching for treasure without a map. Solution criteria are like the landmarks provided by treasure maps. They are the landmarks that lead to the appropriate solution. A treasure map is only as good as its factual accuracy, so too with solution criteria. Solution criteria are not a matter of preference or opinion but specific descriptors that identify the elements of the solution. They are the standards by which the solution can be chosen.

> By choosing our path, we choose our destination.
>
> —Unknown

Not having a procedure for solving the problem will lead to either an unintended odyssey or to a wrong solution, quite likely both.

Choosing the wrong problem-solving process is like trying to "jam a square peg into a round hole" or trying to solve a division problem using addition. As shown by these two examples, the solution process must fit the problem in question. The rational problem-solving techniques explained in this chapter are *action planning*, *contingency planning*, *scenario development*, and *imaging*.

Pay close attention to the accuracy, the application of the criteria, and the choice and execution of the problem-solving strategy. Due diligence here will not only guarantee finding a quality solution but also save much time and energy. When groups fail to consider rational solution criteria or a rational procedure for seeking solutions to problems, many crazy, unproductive things can happen. Here are some that appear quite frequently.

# Foibles and Fumbles While Setting Solution Criteria and Selecting a Problem-Solving Procedure

Solution criteria are the standards by which a judgment or decision can be made. They should be clear, understandable, relative to the problem itself, fair and reasonable, and finally, realistic. They should be the yardsticks that accurately measure the elements of a successful solution. Sometimes groups disregard or lose sight of these facts and deviate from the rational.

## The Warm Fuzzy

Mary Poppins is alive and well. For this group, the criteria for solutions to problems are based on the premise that "a spoonful of sugar makes the medicine go down." Cute quick fixes are always in high demand with this group. Perhaps by feeling good, the problem will want to go away on its own. While the symbolism and feeling tone generated by these well-meaning gestures are laudatory, they seldom get to the core of the problem, and more likely, they just mask the symptoms.

# The Turducken (Previously Known as the Three-Bird Roast)

Rather than a single fumble, *the Turducken* represents a classification of fumbling. As the name implies, there are various ways of stuffing solutions inside each other or adding one indiscriminate solution on top of another. Here are some:

- *Two From Column 1, One From Column 2*

    Its premise is "more is better," and if you include "everything but the kitchen sink," you're probably going to hit something, maybe even a solution. So elements of a solution are indiscriminately chosen based on people's opinions. "Our solution should have one of those, two of these, four of those, and don't forget to include one of them." All the chefs are in the kitchen, and the ingredients multiply.

- *The Blue Ribbon Approach*

    This is the favorite of "select committees" everywhere. Rather than taking the thoughtful step of developing a concise and coherent set of criteria, this gathering—of gurus or perhaps influencers—believes each of their utterances should carry weight. Therefore, their every opinion proffered is held sacrosanct. When the gurus speak, everyone listens, and we have the improbable laundry lists of solution criteria to prove it. Does it have practical usefulness? Probably not. It's seldom that ivory tower thinking coincides with real-world doing.

- *The Mutual Admiration Society. Experts Gone a-Rye*

    When this committee meets, it's an event. Elocution is the vehicle as members compete to hear themselves talk. They, rather than the problem, become the focus of the proceedings. They exchange flatteries and promote each other's astute thinking. "But of course, your opinion is important. It must be included as a recommendation." "What can I say, but thank you, and your insightful commentary that should be included." This interplay continues until the members become so flattered they are beside themselves, or time runs out, usually the latter. While the committee might be satisfied with itself, the problem has been sitting in the empty chair during these proceedings. When a problem is not present in the proceedings, it probably hasn't been addressed well.

There have always been two problems with eating *Turducken*—bloating and an upset stomach. A *Turducken* set of criteria does the same thing to problem solving. It usually provides such an excessive list of criteria that the resulting solutions are difficult, if not impossible, to implement. Many *Turducken* solutions don't integrate well. Their incongruities add such confusion and misdirection; they have no real practicality. The *three-bird roast becomes a horse, cow, chicken.* You can't ride it. You can't milk it. And it doesn't lay eggs.

## Let Mikey Do It

It's not our responsibility. It's not politically feasible. This is a process of passing the problem to someone else. The procedure for solving a problem in this case is either done by kicking the problem upstairs to be solved or kicking it downstairs by delegating it to a subpart of the school's organization. It's a counseling problem. The English department can do it. The kindergarten staff has time. It's an HR problem. Passing the buck is an extremely easy tactic but rarely provides an effective outcome.

Regularly used by dependent groups is the Oracle of Delphi, a.k.a., *Sit With the Guru*. This group always wants to bring in an expert to solve problems. After an appropriate display of hero worship, a solution is proffered by the seer, becomes doctrine, and is accepted by the group as an act of faith, fear, or fatigue. Many times, cults of followers are the residue of this experience. An enjoiner here. Bringing an expert in to assist, train, or mentor a group with a pre-identified need for knowledge or skill is not to be confused with the *Let Mikey's Do It* strategy. The first is group development, the second is group abrogation.

## Putting It All Together: Set the Solution Criteria and Find Solution Alternatives

**Figure 5.1** Setting the Course to the Solution

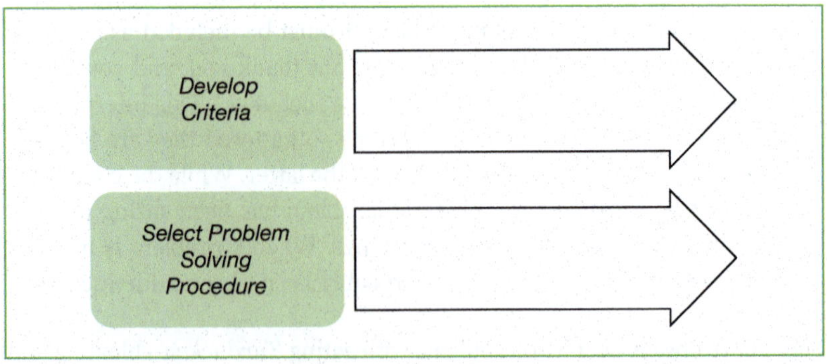

*Develop Criteria*

*Select Problem Solving Procedure*

To set the proper course to a destination, one needs to pinpoint the location of the destination, then determine the best way to get there (Figure 5.1). Setting the course to a good solution requires pinpointing "the where" of the solution-developing definitive solution criteria and "the how" to get there—identifying the appropriate solution procedure. The following two tasks build that course.

# Task 1: Develop Solution Criteria

"You can't tell the players without a scorecard," as the old baseball adage goes. Consider this. The problem solvers have found a number of possible solutions. However, they have neglected to develop a common understanding of the elements that constitute an acceptable choice. The group now must decide which of the options should be selected as the solution. How should they rationally proceed? Without a predefined yardstick, choosing a solution now becomes a reactive process, often an emotional interaction. Judging usually turns into advocating. Having no common standard, group members champion their favorite. The rules for selecting a solution are made on the fly, if made at all. The result usually ends up with the selection process becoming some version of a Foible or Fumble. Developing selection standards beforehand predefines the decision-making parameters. Having a predetermined yardstick enables decision-making to be conducted as a thoughtful conversation rather than a raucous free-for-all. Avoiding a free-for-all at this critical juncture is a good idea and worth the effort.

Three parts make up a solution criterion, the *descriptor*, *priority*, and *standard of measurement*.

1. **Descriptor** describes or identifies a central or important attribute of the solution. Descriptors can be a component, an action, or a result of the solution.

    - A *component* is a particular actor or discerning element of the solution.
    - An *action* is a process or procedure of the solution.
    - A *result* is the expected outcome or conclusion produced by the solution.

2. **Priority** describes its worth for inclusion in the solution. Priorities are either a *must*, a *prefer*, or a *nice to*.

    - A *must* is an essential, a necessity, or a fundamental element of the solution. It is a requirement of any solution.
    - A *prefer* is the acceptable choice of alternatives in a solution.
    - A *nice to* is an element that is desirable but not essential.

3. **Standard** is the performance statement of the required outcome of the end state.

    - The *benchmark* identifies the category or item by which the descriptor is measured.
    - *Measure* describes the degree to which the descriptor is present. Quantitative numerically measures the size, amount, or degree of the descriptor's presence. Qualitative

measurement recounts or describes the knowledge, experience, skill, behavior, or attitude of the descriptor.

– *Indicant* states the level of change or degree of success required.

Here's a simple example of a solution criterion. The problem identified is a budget shortfall. Two solution criteria might look like this:

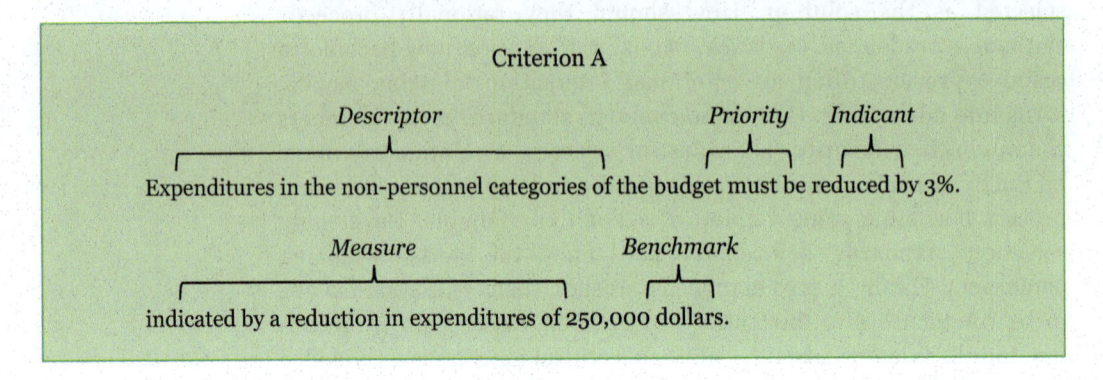

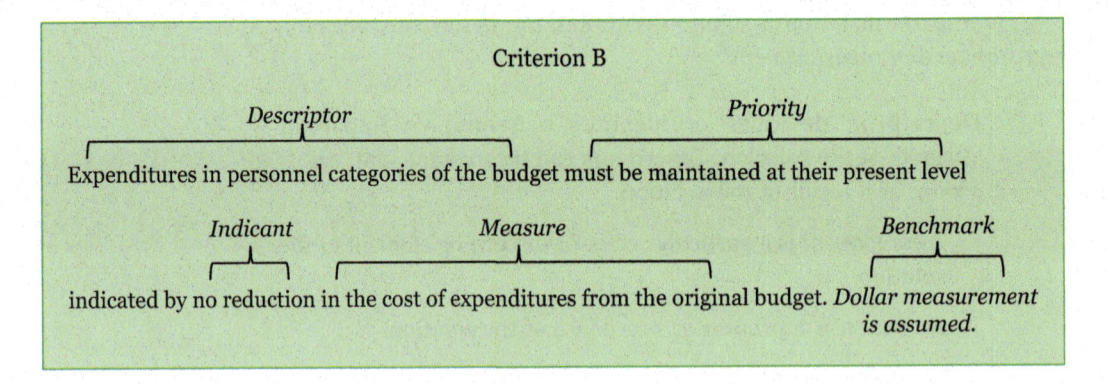

---

**Criterion A**

*Descriptor* / *Priority* / *Indicant*

Expenditures in the non-personnel categories of the budget must be reduced by 3%.

*Measure* / *Benchmark*

indicated by a reduction in expenditures of 250,000 dollars.

---

**Criterion B**

*Descriptor* / *Priority*

Expenditures in personnel categories of the budget must be maintained at their present level

*Indicant* / *Measure* / *Benchmark*

indicated by no reduction in the cost of expenditures from the original budget. *Dollar measurement is assumed.*

---

▸ Notice criteria express the end state of the solution, those parts of original situation that must or should be included, as well as the changes required. The development of criteria depends on the nature of the problem and how stakeholders choose to frame the criteria for success.

When writing, keep the following in mind. Quality criteria statements are relevant, precise, understandable, and discerning. They are

▸ Relevant: They describe the essential attributes of the solution.

▸ Precise: They are exact in their phrasing; they clearly define what the solution is and isn't.

▸ Understandable: They use language that accurately expresses the idea while being clearly understood by the stakeholders.

▸ Discerning: They provide a definitive yardstick to assess and judge competing alternatives.

## Developing Criteria

> ▶ *Rule 9. Put the time in at the front end to avoid headaches at the back end. Do what is necessary to build a complete set of solution criteria and ensure the criteria are understood and agreed to by the stakeholder group.*

The role of solution criteria cannot be overemphasized. They may be the most important tool used in the problem-solving process. Solution criteria are the qualifiers that determine the solution. The better the qualifier, the better the solution.

> **Theoretical Connections**
>
> For a more detailed understanding of this concept, see Chapter 16 of *Making Tough Decisions* (1990) by Paul Nutt.

*Task. Develop Solution Criteria.*
Make sure the stakeholder group fully understands that solution criteria lead to good solutions. Here is an example of what happens when this isn't the case.

A group of old friends haven't seen each other in a long time. Texting, they decide to meet for dinner two weeks from now. The group planner—there is always one member who automatically volunteers—says she will make the arrangements. She asks the group for suggestions for a restaurant and food preferences. As can happen, responses are either vague or conflicting: "Oh, you decide." "I'm good with anything." Other replies are very specific: "I'm a Vegan." "I'm a big steak fan." "Let's do Greek." Working from the comments, the group planner tries to accommodate everyone's wishes. She finds a restaurant that can seat the group, but the reservation opening is earlier than preferred. The restaurant's menu has meat and vegan entrees. They even feature a Greek salad. It's the best option available. She books it and notifies the group. Due to the change in meeting time, one person cancels. Another is disgruntled because parking costs too much. The group has dinner, and while they were glad to meet, they are upset by the meal. They comment, "Service was terrible." "The prices were far too high." "The restaurant was so noisy; we couldn't hear each other talk."

What happened? Those preferences that were voiced were considered. Those preferences like price, ambiance, or a specific timeframe were not voiced so were not considered. If the group had been more reflective and provided clear and comprehensive feedback about preferred choices, the event would have turned out very differently. Shakespeare said it well: "Wisely and slow; they stumble that run fast."

This task will most likely take more time than the group may want to devote to it. Creating the descriptors, priorities, and standards required to evaluate a solution takes time and reflection. While the process may feel slow, the deliberateness it creates avoids stumbling.

## Keeping Tabs on Criteria Building

Figure 5.2 illustrates a way of visualizing and recording the development of solution criteria. Make this spreadsheet the centerpiece of the generating process. The visual will draw the group's attention to the three elements of a criterion and make the specifics of a criterion easier to understand. Provide examples to learn from, and keep an easy tally, avoiding duplicates. It will keep the group on track. Here's how it works.

**Figure 5.2** A Spreadsheet Charting the Elements of Solution Criteria

|  | Element 1. *Descriptor* | | | Element 2. *Priority* | | | Element 3. *Standard* | | |
| --- | --- | --- | --- | --- | --- | --- | --- | --- | --- |
|  | Component | Action | Result | Must | Prefer | Nice to | Benchmark | Measure | Indicant |
| Criterion 1 | | | | | | | | | |
| | | | | | | | | | |
| | | | | | | | | | |
| | | | | | | | | | |
| | | | | | | | | | |

The chart depicts the three parts of a quality criterion: descriptor, priority, and standard. Creating criteria begins with having a working knowledge of a *solution statement*.

*Task 1. Image a solution.* (See the previous chapter.) Start the task by parsing out the descriptors represented by 5Ws in the solution statement. Then write a simple declarative statement for each descriptor, identifying it as either a component, action, or outcome. Transcribe each descriptor to the Criteria Spreadsheet flipchart. Once done, statements are revised to create the final list. The group then decides the priority for each criterion, and a checkmark is placed in either the *Must*, *Prefer*, or *Nice To* column accordingly. Finally, a standard is developed for each descriptor.

Have the group work on one criterion at a time.

Here (in Figure 5.3) is an example of a criterion being transcribed to the Solution Criteria Spreadsheet. Criterion B, *expenditures in personnel categories of the budget must be maintained at their present level indicated by no reduction in the cost of expenditures from the original budget.* This is how it could be transcribed to the spreadsheet.

**Figure 5.3** Listing Criterion

|  | Element 1. Descriptor ||| Element 2. Priority ||| Element 3. Standard |||
|---|---|---|---|---|---|---|---|---|---|
|  | Component | Action | Result | Must | Prefer | Nice to | Benchmark | Measure | Indicant |
| Criterion |  |  | Expenditures in personnel categories remain the same. | X |  |  | Amount in $. | Cost of personnel expenditures. | No reduction. |

The following qualifiers can be used to guide members when creating criterion. Each criterion should be:

- *Clearly written.* It should be clearly stated in language that is understood by the stakeholders. It should be a specific and an essential element of the solution.

- *Discriminating.* The statement should discern what the solution contains and doesn't contain. The yardsticks and descriptions of the end state must be unambiguous.

- *Specific.* The measurement for success is definite and specific.

- *Supportable.* Each criterion is on point. Each measures some aspect of the solution.

- *Realistic.* The required end state for each criterion is attainable and represents an outcome required of the solution.

## TASK CUE CARD

- *Desired Outcome:* A comprehensive list of solution criteria has been developed.

- *Group Organizers: Whip Around, Combining and Winnowing, Spend-a Dot, Triads,* and *Straw Polling*

- *Your Team Lesson Plan:* Before the meeting, provide group members with study materials covering the solution criteria. Provide particular support for the difficult aspects of formulating criteria. Provide cheat sheets explaining the most effective qualitative and quantitative procedures.

- Use three flipcharts for this task. Attach the *Solution Statement* to Flipchart 1. Attach the *Solution Criteria Spreadsheet* to Flipchart 2. Post the *Criterion Qualifiers* to Flipchart 3.

- Begin the meeting by discussing the importance of the agenda and the benefit of the desired outcome. Explain the task using the charts as visuals.

- Check for Understanding. Explain *description*, *priority*, and *standard*, and allow the group the opportunity to question for clarification and further definition. Ensure all members have a working understanding of *descriptors, priority* levels, and *standards*.

- Referring to the *Solution Image Statement* on Flipchart 1, have the group review the statement for clarification.

- Next, do one or two practice rounds. Give the group members a minute or two to identify a descriptor. Ask a member to volunteer an example. Copy it to the flipchart. Next, have group members volunteer revisions and improvements using the posted qualifiers. Once completed, have members determine the criterion's priority level. Finally, in open group discussion, have the members determine the benchmark category, measure, and indicant for the criterion. Do a second round. (*The preceding exercise can be used as a stand-alone training session, if needed.*)

- Provide the group with thinking time to individually identify descriptors. Do a *Whip-Around,* posting descriptors from each member, combining and revising as you go, until the list is completed. Using the *Spend-a-Dot*, green dots only, have each group member select a priority level for each descriptor by placing a dot in the designated column. Tally each column. Determine the priority level for each descriptor Where votes are split, discuss and come to agreement.

- Take a 5- to 15-minute break.

- Bring the group back in session. Do a quick review of what has been completed so far. Do a check for understanding on the elements of a criterion standard. Now break the group into triads. Have each triad develop a standard for each criterion. When groups are done, have them post their results on flipcharts and post them in the front of the room. Do a clarifying, combining, and winnowing exercise with the posted standards. Where there are competing standards for a criterion, either do a straw vote to determine the group's preference or keep both standards, where reasonable.

- Have a writing team compile the criterion into a publishable form and distribute to the group.

- The estimated time to complete this task is 1–3 hours. The task can be broken down into multiple segments if needed. Descriptors can be developed as homework to shorten the process. Triads could also work on standards to shorten the process.

# Task 2: Select a Problem-Solving Procedure

In arithmetic, processes of subtraction or division are not used to add things together, nor are the processes of addition or multiplication used to divide things from each other. To work, these processes must be correctly applied. Humans have been inventing procedures to simplify and speed up how we think and do since the discovery of fire and the invention of the wheel. As Thomas Carlyle so aptly put it, "Man is a tool-using animal. Without tools he is nothing; with tools he is all." The key is learning to use the right tool for the job. The tool doesn't work if a hammer is used when a saw is required.

So it is with problem solving and decision-making. The appropriate mental tools must be employed to solve the problem. Brainstorming doesn't work well when trying to filter or pare things down, and winnowing and combining things doesn't work when trying explore all possibilities. The success of all problem solving is largely dependent on what mental tools—what procedures—are used to reach the solution.

The key to finding the right procedure for handling a problem is understanding its level of difficulty. For instance, a problem could emerge as one of two or more entirely different scenarios. In this case, a problem-solving procedure that accounts for only solution alternative won't suffice. Using procedural thinking that adds costs to a deficit situation is probably a bad idea too. Here's the next rule:

> **Rule 10.** *The problem determines how it needs to be solved, not the other way around. The procedure for solving a problem is based on the nature and difficulty of the problem.*

There are many procedures available to work out problems.

The solution procedures presented in the text have been selected because of their ease of use and their effectiveness at addressing school problems.

**Figure 5.4** Selecting Problem-Solving Procedures According to Problem Difficulty

|  |  |
|---|---|
| SIMPLE<br>Action Learning | COMPLICATED<br>Contingency Planning |
| COMPLEX<br>Creative Problem Solving | CHAOTIC<br>Crisis Management |

The Cynthia Kurtz and Dave Snowden model illustrates the solution procedure used according to the facts that are known about the problem and the potential solution.

## Simple Problems

As is seen in Figure 5.4. The *simple* problem occupies the upper left quadrant. These problems tend to be overwhelmingly static, predictable, and consistent in how they play out. So, a procedure that can determine the elements of the solution based on the facts known about the problem would work here. The *action-learning procedure* (Figure 5.5) does just that. Action learning is a simple process of reflection, a kind of group meta-cognition.

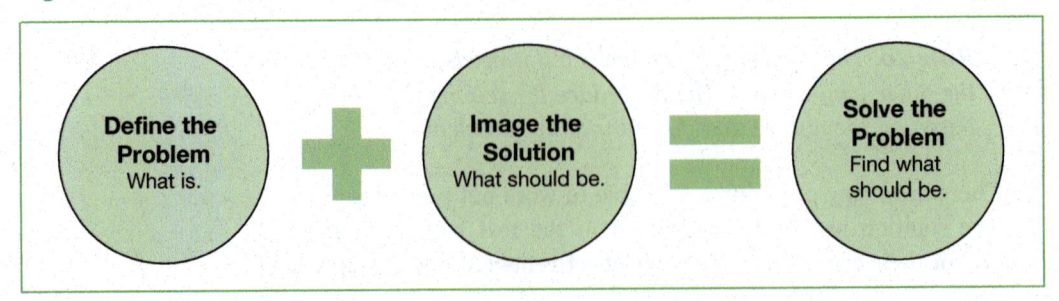

**Figure 5.5** The Action-Learning Procedure

**Define the Problem** What is. **+** **Image the Solution** What should be. **=** **Solve the Problem** Find what should be.

Based on the groundbreaking work of Reg Revan in the United Kingdom, it works like this. Action learning is a three-step process: a reflection on what is, an assessment of what should be, and the building or finding of a solution that satisfies the "should be" conditions. What did we do? How did it work? What do we do next?

> **Theoretical Connections**
>
> For a more academic understanding of this concept, see the seminal work *Action Science* (1985) by Chris Argyris, Robert Putnam, and Diana McLain Smith. For a practical discussion on the subject see *Optimizing the Power of Action Learning* (2018) by Michael Marquardt.

## Complicated Problems

*Complicated problems* are "*If this/Then this*" problems. If this happens, then solution A works, but if this happens, then Solution B works. *Contingency-planning procedures* develop solutions based on the "what ifs." What would the correct solution be if A happens? What would be the correct solution if B happens?

**Figure 5.6** The Contingency Plan Procedure

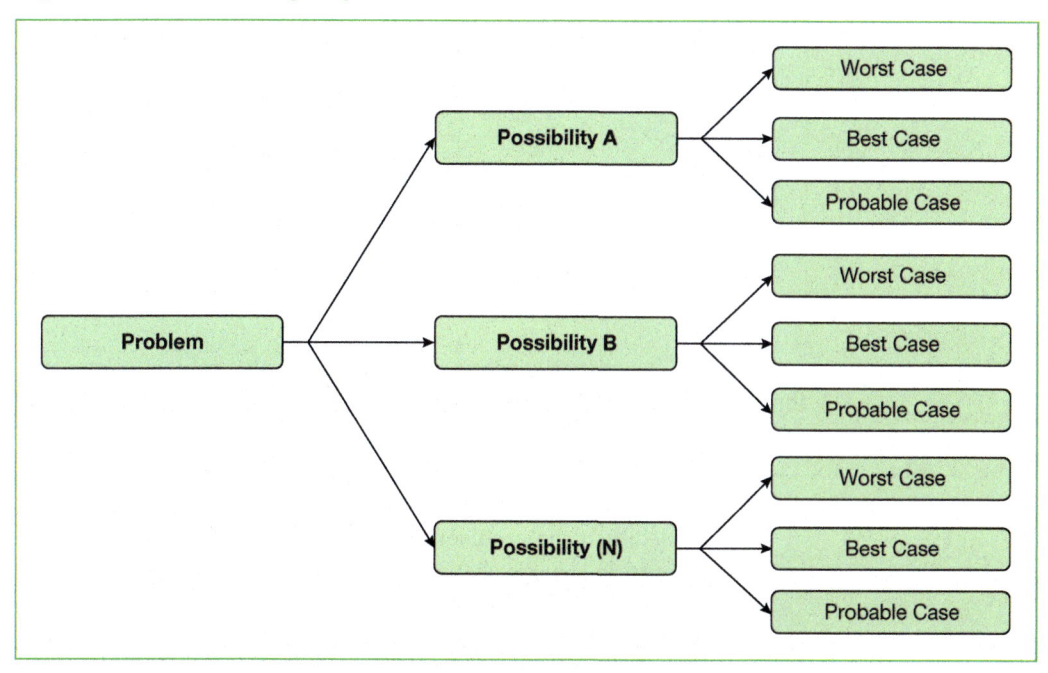

The procedure develops multiple solutions to accommodate the eventualities. *Scenarios, the images of particular "what/if" solutions, are constructed for each contingency.* The *Complicated* problem is best solved by *Contingency Planning* and *Scenario Building* Procedures (Figure 5.6).

> ### Theoretical Connections
>
> For a more academic understanding of what/if thinking see Paul Nutt *Making Tough Decisions* (1990), Chapter 18. For a straight forward presentation of the contingency process see *Contingency Planning* (1981) by Knutson and Alexander. Scenarios are explained in the seminal text *The Art of the Long View* (1996) by Peter Schwartz.

## Complex Problems

The *complex* problem is located in the lower left quadrant. These situations present problems that are ill defined and solutions that are unknown. Their circumstances are entirely new, having little or no association with present experience. The problem and the solution need to be imagined.

**Figure 5.7** The Creative Problem-Solving Procedure

| Discover. | Dream. | Design. | Do. |
|---|---|---|---|
| Clarify what the problem looks like. | Imagine what the solution would look like. | Develop the 5Ws of the dream. | Implement the design. |

Figure 5.7 depicts the process used to creatively problem solve using the 4D process adapted from the work of Osborne and Parnes. Here is how it works.

- *Discover.* Clarify and define the problem. Learn as much as possible about the problem by searching out similar situations from outside sources. Gather salient facts. Construct the problem from what has been learned.

- *Dream.* Using imaging techniques, imagine what the solution would look like. Envision the 5Ws of this new world. Create the picture.

- *Design.* Realize the picture. Construct and develop the structures, procedures, and elements necessary to make the dream a reality.

- *Do.* Implement the action planning necessary to make the design operational.

> **Theoretical Connections**
>
> Here are two texts that provide an in-depth understanding of the creative process: Tony Proctor's (2010) text *Creative Problem Solving for Managers*, and *Futuring: The Exploration of the Future* (2005) by Edward Cornish.

## Chaotic Problems

*Chaotic problems* are unknowns. They occur without warning—those disasters and tragedies that suddenly happen and crash down on an unsuspecting leadership, staff, and community. An on-the-spot *crisis management plan* must be created to react to and to confront the problem. The *chaotic* problem solvers must do damage control and triage the problem, creating solutions while simultaneously trying to deal with the chaos. Figure 5.8 describes a simple problem-solving procedure that can be used for this situation.

**Figure 5.8** Reacting to a Crisis: The 3C Problem-Solving Procedure

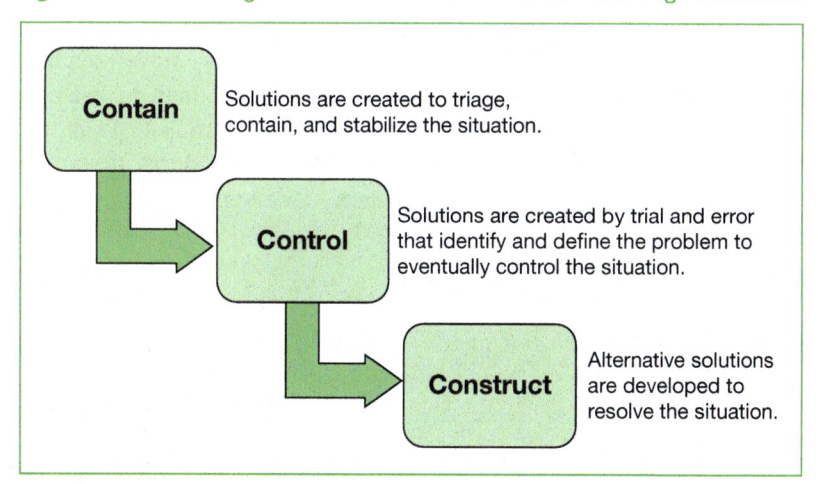

- **Contain**: Solutions are created to triage, contain, and stabilize the situation.
- **Control**: Solutions are created by trial and error that identify and define the problem to eventually control the situation.
- **Construct**: Alternative solutions are developed to resolve the situation.

As shown in the graphic, the stakeholder group follows a three-phase procedure to react to the situation:

- *Contain.* First, solutions are created to assess the type and urgency of the problem, and solutions are developed to temporarily contain and stabilize the situation.

- *Control.* Second, solutions are developed using trial and error, bootstrapping techniques to identify and define the problem situation. Once identified, solutions evolve until the situation is controlled.

- *Construct.* Third, using the findings of the second phase as foundation knowledge, solution criteria are generated, alternative solutions are collected, and a solution or solutions are chosen to resolve the situation.

Each problem situation is unique in time and space. Some are more familiar than others. Some are simple and straightforward. Their solutions come easily, while others are very complex, multifaceted problems, requiring more than one solution to resolve the situation.

Four simple problem-solving procedures have been presented here to address the major types and difficulties of problems posed in schools. There are numerous other procedures available. Remember, when choosing a problem-solving procedure, tailor the procedure to the problem. **Remember *Rule 8*.**

## Theoretical Connections

For a more detailed understanding of this concept see *Managing Business Crises* (2002) by John Burnett.

*Task. Select a Problem-Solving Procedure.*
Prior to meeting, send group members the accumulated information on the problem definition, its type, and problem difficulty. Have members also review the solution statement just created. Ask them to examine these materials and think how they might solve the problem. Begin the meeting by explaining the four problem-solving procedures described. Check for understanding. Once common understanding is reached, proceed with the *Lesson Plan*.

## TASK CUE CARD

- *Desired Outcome:* The Group selects the appropriate problem-solving procedure

- *Group Organizers: Spend-a-Dot, Consensus,* and *Action Plan Processes* (see glossary for complete directions for doing *Spend-a-dot* and *Action Plans*.)

- *Your Team Lesson Plan:* Place Figure 5.4 (Select Problem-Solving Procedure), the *Problem Definition Statement,* and the *Problem Solution Statement* on three flipcharts in front of the group. Ensure charts can be easily read by the entire group. Read the problem and solution statements in turn and discuss what is known about the 5Ws of each statement. Record the responses on a flipchart. Next, ask the group what is not known about the 5Ws of each statement. On a separate flipchart, record those responses. Post all responses in plain view.

- Now center the group's attention on Figure 5.4. Explain the quadrants and the requirements for selecting each of the three procedures listed. Check for understanding and clarify as needed.

- Now, explain *Spend-a-Dot.* Distribute 4 green sticky dots and 2 red sticky dots to each group member. Explain the purpose of the dot procedure is the selection of the appropriate *problem-solving procedure.* Using the information contained on the flipcharts, have each member choose the procedure needed to solve the problem by placing (spending) 1 to 4 dots on the appropriate quadrant on Figure 5.4.

- Members are to place the two red sticky dots on one or more of the quadrants whose procedure is inappropriate. Once members have voted their choice, review the results with the group. If there is a consensus, proceed to developing an *Action Plan* for conducting the procedure. If the choice is unclear, use a consensus process to gain group agreement, and then develop an *Action Plan* to move forward. Sample lesson plans for conducting a *discrepancy analysis, contingency planning, the 4Ds* and *3C Crisis Management* are found in the glossary.

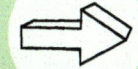

## Consider This . . .

This thought should be obvious, but often it is not. Stop and think. Especially in the case of a crisis, time is important, but so is thinking. Short of events such as the building being on fire, even just a few minutes to consider what action is most likely to produce a needed step toward a solution can make the difference between containing the problem versus making the problem worse and ending up with unwanted outcomes that snowball into an ever-worsening situation.

**CHAPTER 6**

# Define Search Strategies and Find Solution Alternatives

*If you don't know where you are going, any road will get you there.*

—Lewis Carroll (1865)

There are numerous ways to search for a solution. Yogi Berra, a baseball all-time great, was giving his lifelong friend Joe Garagiola directions to his house. When Joe asked Yogi how to get there, he replied: "When you get to the fork in the road; take it."

Not having an appropriate search strategy is much like getting to the fork in the road and taking it. Any old tine will do. There is a good chance of choosing an inappropriate tine, one that can lead to the group taking the wrong road and leading to an unsuitable solution, a search process that has the group wandering aimlessly through confusion leading to a solution chosen by chance.

Not having a good search procedure can lead to either an unintended odyssey or to a wrong solution. Louis Sullivan, the founder of modern of American Architecture, used a maxim that best explains this idea: "Form follows function." The search process is dependent on the problem procedure.

For example, if the purpose of the solution is to come up with a stopgap fix as soon as possible, it's probably unwise to engage in some lengthy creative process to determine the solution. When a fire is raging, holding a committee meeting to discuss the "pros and cons" of how to put out the fire just doesn't cut it.

Knowledge-based, experimental-based, and imagination-based search strategies are explained in this chapter. Since form follows function, the search strategies presented are paired to the requirements of the three problem-solving procedures.

The second topic of this chapter addresses solution alternatives. Here, determining the "hows and whats" of a good solution moves from a general discussion to the specific details for finding viable alternatives and being able to judge their worth.

> **Rule 11.** *Have a clear image of what will solve the problem and a specific route for finding it.*

A quality solution is found by using well defined criteria matched with the right problem-solving procedure. A three-step process details how this is done. This chapter presents the four cases that map connecting the solution criteria to each problem-solving procedure to determine the appropriate search strategies. An Action Plan Template is provided to conclude the chapter.

## Foibles and Fumbles While Defining Search Strategies and Finding Solution Alternatives

### Who Wants to Be a Millionaire

Under this general category are a number of the more prevalent F and Fs. This quiz show format really appeals to those who would rather not do the hard work of methodically finding solution alternatives. These folks would prefer a shortcut while increasing their popularity rating to boot. Instead of rationally trying to solve the problem, they might employ one or more of the following strategies.

> *A variation of the 50–50 Option.* The group brainstorms suggestions for solutions until they can't come up with any more. Then by voicing their personal opinions, they vote alternatives off the island one at a time, until one is left standing.

> *Phone-a-Friend.* Don't want to do the heavy lifting? Here's the ticket. Phone or text a friend. The group presents the problem to a friend or friends, then asks them how they would solve it. The response that's liked best is chosen, and voila. There is a cover your posterior version of this as well. Here, rely on an important person up the food chain. Get his or her recommendation for solving the problem. Implement it. If the problem is solved, credit the caring mentor. The best part is, if the solution goes south, the blame can be discreetly passed on.

CHAPTER 6. Define Search Strategies and Find Solution Alternatives

- *Ask the Audience.* Known as *Survey Says*, this option queries a convenient population to seek alternatives. Different than getting feedback on possible solutions from stakeholders, this option haphazardly frames the problem and asks others to provide the solutions. Whatever the survey says, that's what we do. It can appear as an agenda item at PTAs, school site councils, and the university faculty forums, solution generators all. It's pretty safe too, with admirable transparency, power to the people, and democracy in action. What's happening here is sharing opinions without accounting for any factual credibility or accurate measurement of viability. Sharing ignorance on a large-scale is no more reliable than sharing ignorance on a small scale; the noise is just louder.

- *It's Digital.* With the dawn of the digital age, we have new and improved ways to exchange opinions. They are quick and slick. Why bother using paper or waiting to convene to get the opinion of the masses. We've got Twitter (formally known as X), Facebook, and so forth. How easy this is! Just tweet the problem and get started. Log on to your favorite social media feed, select a group or click the, "What's on Your Mind" icon, and you're ready to rumble. Now, sit back and wait for the responses and mentions to chirp in. If you do it long enough, there's an added advantage. You can garner a large enough following to become an influencer. How great is that? Never mind that you're probably getting haphazard samples from individuals with empty craniums who may very well have axes to grind. Don't worry about the fact that the responses lack credible evidence to back them up. Who'll notice that no effort has been made to ensure common understanding of the problem or what a viable solution might look like? Go with the flow.

- We have now added AI to the lifeline group. Why bother getting into a tizzy about finding solutions. Have the "digital Mikey" do it. After all, "digital Mikey" is probably smarter than any of us. Yup, query the chatbot for solutions. The response will be quick. Reliable? Not so much. Stakeholders included? Who knows?

Before the anticipated blowback and indignant retorts begin, using social media to interact with stakeholders is extremely handy, if done correctly. When the information exchanged is purposeful, authentic, and accurate, then digital querying can be very effective. There are rules however. A digital query must be:

1. *Purposeful*, in that it clearly and concisely addresses the situation; it's on point.

2. *Authentic*, in that it's theoretically or pragmatically well founded. It's based on facts and evidence, not opinion.

3. *Accurate*, in that it represents the response of the entire population. The information is generalizable. It is not based on

some haphazard sample, which seems to be the currency of the day. The opinions of the outraged few do not represent the choices of the many.

### The Tug-of-War

Problem-solving rational solution choices are not the option here. Using that overriding principle of "I'm right, and you're wrong," solution choices are based on the two opposing sides locking horns in battle. There's only one way to understand the solution; we know it, and you don't. This continues until one side blinks or until both sides are forced into a compromise either due to external forces or sheer exhaustion. The heroes of the ordeal are anointed; results are tallied; but the problem itself never gets fully addressed.

The "we/they" groups exist to do the Tug-of-War because it's easier to create an adversarial relationship, since honest mutually beneficial partnerships are hard to build and maintain. The result is confrontation and the forcing of one group's will on another. *It's weapon is not logical reasoning but the ad hominem fallacy attack.*

### Tit for Tat

Searching for solutions is based on the we/they making nice by trading favors, the favorite of our more politically bent crowd. Collaborative solution seeking is replaced by "the little black book." Both the we and the they keep a tally sheet that lists the favors and compromises made by each side to the other. Every time a side gives a favor, it is owed one. This can work when the solution is of mutual benefit to the needs of both parties. If that is the case, why is it a favor or compromise?

## Putting It All Together: Define Search Strategies and Find Solution Alternatives

**Figure 6.1** Finding the Solution

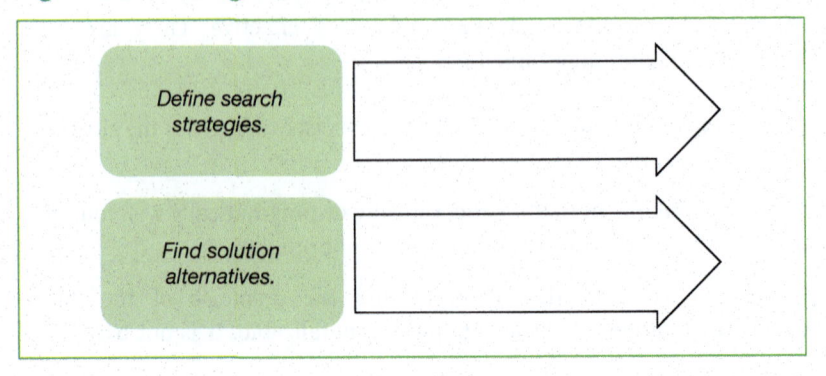

# Task 1: Defining Search Strategies

It's time to find the solution (see Figure 6.1). Which path should be taken? A search strategy provides a specific roadmap to determine which road to take based on the type of solution sought and what is known about it. Choosing the right search strategy not only saves time but will also lead to a better solution. Five basic search strategies are presented in Figure 6.2.

1. The first category along the continuum is *knowledge-based search strategy*. This category is used when knowledge of the problem and the solution is either completely or partially known.

2. The second category is the *experiment-based search strategy*. Here, knowledge of the problem is known or partially known, and the solution is unknown.

3. The third category is the *imagination-based search strategy*. This strategy is used when little or nothing is known about the problem and the solution is unknown.

**Figure 6.2** Search Strategies

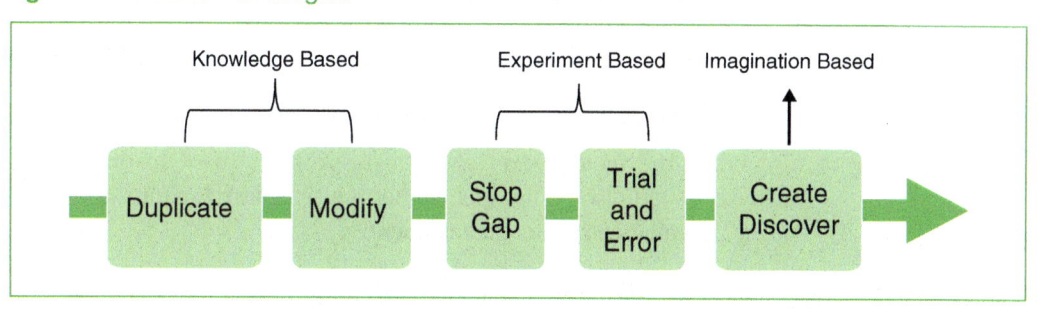

[Diagram: Knowledge Based (Duplicate, Modify) → Experiment Based (Stop Gap, Trial and Error) → Imagination Based (Create Discover)]

The following discussion provides a description and the use for each of the five.

## Theoretical Connections

Richard Lyles's (1982) text *Practical Management Problem Solving and Decision Making*, as well as Chapter 6 and Chapter 9 *of Making Tough Decisions* (1990) by Paul Nutt.

## The Knowledge-Based Searches

*The Duplicate Strategy*. Here is a strategy for finding solution alternatives that match or are equivalent to the solution image. This strategy is tailored to problems where there is much prior knowledge about both the problem and the solution. Since much is generally known about the problem and the solution, competing alternatives are readily available in the field. The duplicate strategy develops a plan to find organizations where a similar problem has occurred and been solved, learn about that solution, and replicate it. Competing alternatives are judged based on their fit with the solution criteria. This is a well-used strategy employed when conducting a discrepancy analysis or in contingency planning.

*The Modification Strategy.* This is the most used knowledge-based strategy. Either the present situation or an alternative is analyzed to determine which of its elements meet the solution criteria. Those elements that do not conform are eliminated, and missing components are created to meet the criteria. The alternative solution is tailored to meet the solution criteria. There are two search strategies here:

- The first is the simplest. After reviewing the solution criteria, analysis shows that a modification of the present situation can solve the problem. Those parts or factors in question are revised, adjusted, or replaced to meet the requirements of the solution criteria.

- The second strategy is a two-step process. In these cases, the initial strategy is a *duplicate strategy*, and a plan is developed to search out possible solutions from other organizations. Once found, the alternatives are analyzed and modified to meet the requirements of the solution criteria.

While the *modification strategy* is primarily used in discrepancy analysis, it can also be used as part of multiple search efforts in contingency planning and crisis management.

## Experiment-Based Searches

*The Stop-Gap Strategy.* This is a makeshift plan that applies a series of improvised fixes to the problem until the situation is temporarily resolved. Here, the problem can be fully or partially known, but the solution is unknown or presently unattainable. Best-bet fixes are applied based on what is known about the problem until the problem's immediate issues are in abeyance. The search strategy is seeking to find a temporary fix. This is the preferred strategy for the control phase in crisis management. The strategy can also be used in contingency planning and discrepancy analysis problem solving where the urgency of the problem requires a stop-gap measure or resources are unavailable to implement the preferred solution.

*The Trial-and-Error Strategy.* This strategy is a practical application of experimental research methods. It begins by searching for a solution that best fits an educated guess of what the problem is. That solution is implemented. Its results are used to frame the next attempt, or trial, to find the solution. Repeated attempts are conducted until the problem is solved. Think of it as the daisy chain approach to searching for a solution. This strategy is used best when a problem is partially known. It can be used in discrepancy analysis. It is the tailored solution for the construct phase in a crisis management problem procedure.

## Imagination-Based Searches

*The Creative/Discover Strategy.* This is the *create a solution from midair* strategy. The plan is completed in three stages: perceiving, imaging, and designing.

- Perceiving: In this first stage, elements of the problem are recognized and identified by comparing the situation to known problems that are similar, applicable metaphors, or the result of brainstorming activities.

- Imaging: The second stage imagines the "end state," the future where the solution has been acted on. The image created provides the picture from which the solution is designed.

- Designing: In the third stage, plans are created that realize the development and implementation of the image created in the previous step. This strategy is used when creating new ventures and requires a substantial amount of time to execute. A comprehensive discussion on this strategy's procedures is covered in the glossary as the P.I.D. Process.

## Task 2: Find Solution Alternatives

Finding good solutions and the effort it takes to uncover them depends on the search strategy used. Choosing a search strategy is not a matter of chance, convenience, or familiarity. The strategy is determined by the *problem-solving procedure* and the *solution criteria*, see Figure 6.3. The *problem-solving procedure* chooses "the how" of the search. The 5Ws and *problem type paired with the solution criteria* determine "the what" of the search. The guesswork has been eliminated. Searching for and finding solutions is a matter of applying what is known. Here is how it works.

### Theoretical Connections

James Higgins provides tools for generating solution alternatives in Chapter 5, *101 Creative Problem-Solving Techniques* (2006).

*Task. Search for Solutions.*
The formula for searching for solutions is a simple three-step process.

**Figure 6.3** The Formula for Searching for Solutions

```
                                    Problem-      • Action Learning
                                    Solving       • Contingency Planning
                                    Procedure     • Crisis Management
                                        │
                                        ▼
         ⎡ • Deficit/Deficiency    ⎤                         • Trial and Error
         ⎢ • Sequential Improvement⎥  Solution  →  Search    • Knowledge Based
  5W's ──⎨ • Emerging Opportunity  ⎬   Image       Process   • Creative Discovery
         ⎣ • New Undertaking       ⎦                         • Stop Gap
                                        │
                                        ▼
                                    Solution
                                    Candidates
```

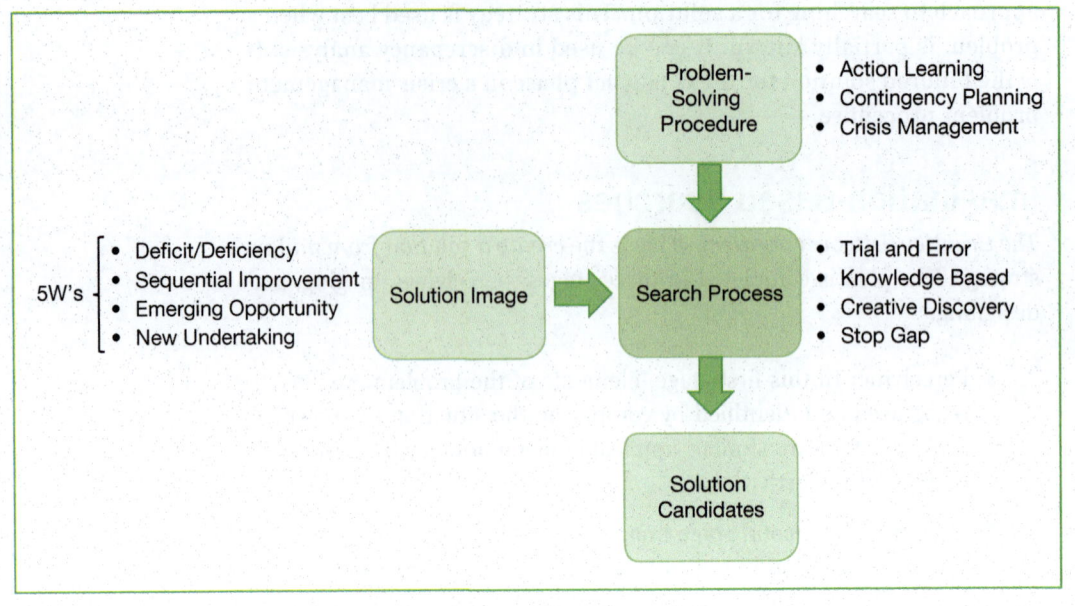

▸ *Step 1: Identify the Problem–Solution Procedure.*

Each of the *problem-solving procedures* presents a very different process (or processes) to follow from the simple *action learning*, where a search strategy is employed to duplicate a known solution, to a *crisis management procedure*, where multiple search strategies are used during each phase of the three-tiered process. Based on the *problem definition*, one of the four procedures is chosen. *Review its processes and select the search strategy or all of the strategies that apply. List the strategies chosen.*

▸ *Step 2: Match the Problem-Solving Procedure With the Solution Image.*

The *5Ws, problem type, and solution criteria* provide the specifics for what the search is looking for. *Using the elements of the solution image, choose the appropriate search strategy or strategies from the list compiled in Step 1.*

▸ *Step 3: Develop an Action Plan to Carry Out the Search Strategies.*

Knowing the specific *problem-solving procedure, solution selection criteria, and search strategy,* develop an action plan to conduct the search. Determine the specific search outcomes, the persons involved in the search process, the resources necessary to conduct the search, and timeline for completion. Execute.

**Rule 12.** *Match the appropriate problem-solving procedure to the stated problem. Each of the four problem-solving procedures is unique.*

CHAPTER 6. Define Search Strategies and Find Solution Alternatives    95

*Choosing the wrong one is having the group fly by the seat of its pants and will crash the airplane.*

The following cases provide a template for how the formula is applied for each *problem-solving procedure*. These cases present a step-by-step outline that can be used to sort out the various search strategies based the type of problem being encountered.

## The Four Cases

Each of the *problem-solving procedures*, as shown in Figure 6.4, are presented as cases. *Action Learning, Contingency Planning and Crisis Management* cover the broad range of day-to-day situations that occur in schools. These situations are either *transactional* problems that require adjusting the way things are done, such as adopting new textbooks or reforming the morning cue for student drop-offs. They can also apply to those *transitional* situations where some type of reform in structure is required, such as moving from a K–8 school configuration to a K–5/6–8 configuration or moving from a semester to a quarter system.

However, transformational situations can occur in a school setting as well. These problems require a radically different way thinking about problems and seeking solutions. The *Creative Problem-Solving* procedure is used for *transformational* situations. Think of a transformational problem as moving from only knowing about transporting by boat or train to trying to figure out how to invent traveling by plane. New ventures like starting a school district, establishing a new college, or eliminating the

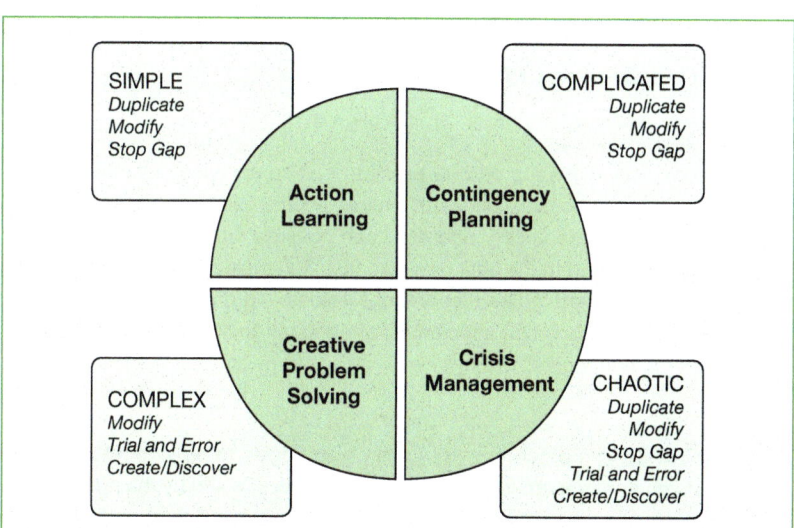

**Figure 6.4** The Search Strategies Used With Problem-Solving Procedures

SIMPLE
*Duplicate*
*Modify*
*Stop Gap*

COMPLICATED
*Duplicate*
*Modify*
*Stop Gap*

COMPLEX
*Modify*
*Trial and Error*
*Create/Discover*

CHAOTIC
*Duplicate*
*Modify*
*Stop Gap*
*Trial and Error*
*Create/Discover*

**Action Learning**  **Contingency Planning**
**Creative Problem Solving**  **Crisis Management**

grade level structure in favor of an open school are all transformational problems. Transformational problem solving uses *imagination-based search strategies*.

The following case templates briefly describe how the formula is applied for each problem-solving procedure. Step 1 provides a brief definition of the procedure. Step 2 suggests the problem types that fit the procedure. Search strategies are then recommended based on the particulars of the problem.

### Case 1. Action Learning.

*Step 1*

Action learning analyzes the situation by asking the following questions: What was done? How did it work? What is to be done next? Discrepancy analysis is used to examine the differences between the desired solution state and the problem situation, identifying where the discrepancy or gap exists.

*Step 2*

It is the preferred procedure for use in solving *deficit/deficiency* and *sequential improvement* problems. *Action learning* can also be used with *Emerging Opportunities* and *New Undertakings* when Blue Skying a problem.

- Search Strategies
- Duplication: This strategy is appropriate when the solution options are clearly known and meet all the standards of the solution criteria.
- Modification: This strategy is appropriate when the solution options are clearly known and meet the *must*-level priorities, while being able to be adjusted and revised to meet the *prefer* and *nice to* priorities.
- Stopgap: This strategy can be used when the solution options are clearly known, but the solution criteria cannot be completely satisfied due to a lack of resources. A solution is pieced together as a temporary measure until adequate resources are available.

### Case 2. Contingency Planning.

*Step 1*

*Contingency planning* is a proactive procedure. Also applying *discrepancy analysis*, it identifies possible alternative future events and prepares solutions for each. *Scenarios* are built to address each possible situation, building solutions that respond to the best or worst case. Examples of problems using this procedure are earthquake preparedness plans and a potential budget deficiency situation. Solution alternatives are chosen to meet the situation when the problem occurs.

*Step 2*

This problem-solving procedure uses search strategies to provide solutions that anticipate and prepare for the various possibilities posed by the problem. The *complicated problem* is best solved by *contingency planning* and *scenario-building procedures*.

*Search Strategies*

The use of strategies is dependent on each envisioned *solution image*. If the anticipated problem is one that has occurred before, then duplication or a modification strategy would be in order. In the case of the potential budget deficiency example, modifications can be made based on monetary standards. So a modification strategy would work. However, consider the problem of earthquake preparedness where modifications could be made based on different futures. Here, probable worst- or best-case scenarios can be developed.

- Duplication: This strategy is appropriate when the solution options of the anticipated problem are clearly known and meet all the standards of the solution criteria.
- Modification: This strategy is appropriate when the anticipated solution options are clearly known. Modifications are revised to meet the degree or amount of change anticipated as the problem changes.
- Stopgap: This strategy can be used when the anticipated solution options are clearly known but the solution criteria cannot be completely satisfied due to a lack of time or resources. A solution is pieced together as a temporary measure until adequate resources are available.

## Case 3. Creative Problem Solving

*Step 1*

Creative problem-solving is also a proactive procedure. Each step of the 4D process requires a different analysis. When discovering, use discrepancy analysis to help in uncovering appropriate outside similar situations for comparison and inclusion for the clarification of the problem. The *dream and design* steps follow the P.I.D. process. The final step, *doing*, uses action planning procedures.

*Step 2*

This problem-solving procedure uses search strategies to provide solutions that anticipate and prepare for the various possibilities posed by the problem. The complex problem is best solved by *discrepancy analysis, the P.I.D. process, and action learning*

*Search Strategies*

The use of strategies is dependent on each of the 4D steps.
- Modification: This strategy is appropriate when trying to discover and define the problem.
- Perceiving, imaging, and designing: This process is used to create the solution.
- Trial-and-error: This strategy is used as an action learning process using iterative attempts to create and prefect the design. Each try is altered based on what has been learned until the solution is realized.

## Case 4. Crisis Management

*Step 1*

The discrepancy analysis procedure is recommended. However, it is applied differently for each stage of the process. Examine the difference between the desired solution state and the actual situation. Once identified, develop a temporary solution to neutralize the effects of the problem. Then, discover where the specific elements causing the discrepancy, or gap, exist. Set the solution image and standards, and build or create the solution.

*Step 2*

This strategy is used when disasters and tragedies suddenly happen. An on-the-spot *crisis management plan* must be created to react to and confront the problem. Problem solvers have to define the problem while simultaneously trying to solve it. The crisis management plan is executed in three stages: *Contain, control, and construct*. All five of the search strategies can used according to the procedure stage.

*Search Strategies*

**Contain**

- Stopgap: This strategy is preferred since the solution, the return to normalcy occurring prior to the situation, is known. A solution is pieced together as a temporary measure until the problem has been defined and solutions have been found.
- Modification: This strategy is appropriate when stopgap solution options are clearly known and meet the *must*-level priorities of a condition of normalcy. This temporary fix remains until the permanent solution is found.

**Control**

- Trial-and-error: This strategy tries various repeated and varied attempts at solving the problem based on educated guesses. Each try is altered based on what has been learned until a solution is found.
- Modification: This strategy is appropriate as a *trial-and-error* option when educated guesses can be associated with a solution. Modifications are revised to meet the standards of the educated guess.

**Construct**

- Duplication: This strategy is appropriate when the solution options found during the *control* phase are clearly known and meet all the standards of the solution criteria.
- Modification: This strategy is appropriate when the solution options found during *construct* are partially known and the *must* priorities of the solution criteria are met. Modifications are made to the solution to include the *prefer* and the *nice to* priorities by trial and error until essential conditions are met.

*Task. Develop and Implement the Action Plan.*

It's time to go to work. Each of the previously described four cases laid out the strategic procedures and specific search strategies needed to find and produce a solution. A problem such as a budget deficit might employ a very simple discrepancy analysis using a duplication search process. This search strategy can be easily accomplished by one person in a short time. In this case, there is probably no need for a formal action plan.

However, contingency planning, crisis management, and creative problem solving can involve lengthy and complicated search processes. In these cases, taking time to determine the who, what, when, and how searches are to be conducted makes good sense. This is particularly the case when dealing with a workgroup.

The benefit of action planning allows the group to break down the search processes into actionable steps that can be easily accomplished and understood. Action planning also allows the group to distribute the necessary resources to conduct searches in a comprehensive way. Finally, action planning addresses timelines and member responsibilities for carrying out searches. The Is are dotted, and the Ts are crossed. Having the group action plan also provides transparency showing how solutions are produced, which will bolster group confidence in the alternatives found when it comes time to choose a solution. Taking the time to get it right here will ensure the search will produce the best results. Action planning is a collaborative process, which results in documenting the specific way forward when conducting the search. The graphic that follows depicts the elements of an action plan.

An action plan begins by identifying the task or tasks needed to be accomplished. Once identified, individuals are assigned to carry out the tasks, and a lead person is assigned to oversee task completion. Necessary resources are allocated for the group to conduct their work, and accountability measures are assigned to ensure search quality. Finally, a timeframe is agreed to for task completion (Figure 6.5).

**Figure 6.5** An Action Plan Template

| Action to Be Completed | Key People Involved | Lead Person | Resources Required | Evaluation Requirements | Timeframe | When Completed |
|---|---|---|---|---|---|---|
| | | | | | | |

## TASK CUE CARD

- *Desired Outcome:* Search strategies produce quality solution alternatives.

- *Group Organizers: Action Plan* and *Thumbs-Up Processes*

- *Your Team Lesson Plan:* As part of meeting preparation, have copies of the chosen solution procedure steps—*that is, Action Learning, Contingency Planning, Creative Problem-Solving,* or *Crisis Management*—available for all participants. Also have the selected search strategies available.

- Post a copy of the *Action Plan Template* on a flipchart where all members can see it easily.

- Begin the meeting by explaining the purpose and the procedure for using an *action plan.* Review each category on the template. Ask for questions and qualifications. Ensure all members understand the elements of an action plan.

- Start by having members identify each search task required to be accomplished. Post each item in the column titled "Action to Be Completed." Make sure each post clearly defines the task to be done.

- Now go to the second column and identify all the people charged with that task. Post their names.

- In the third column, identify the individual who is assigned responsibility for task completion.

- In the "Resources Required" column, determine the resources needed to complete the task—that is, money, materials, facilities, and so forth. List these specifics in this column.

- In the evaluation column, determine the accountability elements required to ensure that the search process and solution procedure are correctly adhered to.

- Agree on the timeframe for completion. List the beginning and end dates.

- The "When Completed" column can be used to set a deadline or be used as a check-off when the task is completed.

- Once all search tasks are completed, have the group review the posted material. Call for questions and clarification. Once done, do a thumbs-up or down to approve the action plan. The estimated time of completion for this activity is 30–90 minutes, depending on the complexity of the problem-solving procedure.

The work group has now completed and agreed to an action plan to search for solutions. The group now sets meeting dates to review progress according to the action plan requirements until the search process is completed and until viable solutions have been determined.

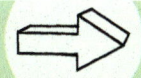

## Consider This...

Have you ever had the experience of having an excellent thought only to lose it when another three things demand your attention? Strategies and alternatives are also called *thinking*. These two steps are not the considerations times, aside from crisis management, to try to rush the results. Remind the team members that some quiet alone time needs to be spent in thought. Actual meeting time is decision-making time, but great thoughts can pop up at any time and need to be recorded before they vanish into the rush of the work day.

**CHAPTER 7**

# Weigh the Alternatives and Decide on a Solution

The most difficult thing is the decision to act!

—Amelia Earhart

Deficiency in decision-making ranks much higher than lack of specific knowledge or technical know-how as an indicator of leadership failure.

—John C. Maxwell

At some point, a decision must be made to solve a problem. The word *decision*'s roots come from the Latin word *decidere*, which means to cut down. Decision-making then is making a judgment by cutting alternatives away in favor of one choice. Knowing how and where to cut solution options will shape the quality and accuracy of the decision, the making of the right choice. This can be a daunting task for the unprepared.

Following the steps of the problem-solving process takes the guesswork out of deciding. To this point, the problem-solving group has used procedures, criteria, and search strategies designed to home in on the appropriate solution options. All that is left now is to choose the right one. As with the earlier efforts, a sound decision-making plan will facilitate the group's ability to weigh the alternatives and find the appropriate solution.

Begin by clearly defining the decision-maker and the role the problem-solving group has in the decision. Next, use the predetermined solution criteria to begin the analytical process that is agreed to for evaluating the worth of each alternative. Finally, select a formal selection process for making the decision. Once the group has agreed to these decision-making parameters, decision-making is accomplished in two steps:

1. The group uses the chosen rating system to evaluate each alternative and select the best.

2. The group agrees to implement the solution chosen, ensuring members have a common understanding of the solution specifics.

Sounds simple enough, and it is, if the problem-solving rules are followed. If the stakeholder group has been involved from the onset, then there has been agreement on:

- the nature of the problem and the nature of the possible solution,
- the criteria for judging the best solution alternative, and
- an agreement on the procedures for searching for solutions.

By now, the group should be of one mind. The group is now armed with criteria that takes the guesswork and personal biases out of the decision-making. This should also lead to the selection of an appropriate solution. However, in the real-world of schools, this rational way of group problem solving is not always the course of action—far from it. Here are a few examples that demonstrate how decision-making can run aground.

## Foibles and Fumbles While Weighing Alternatives and Deciding on a Solution

When decisions need to be made, ego and biases can come to the forefront, and the wielding of power becomes the only way to decide. All the previous work done to rationally find a solution is at best informative—but now comes the serious part. With that thinking, group decision-making can go out the window. The bad news about this highjacking is twofold. First, the decision made will most likely not be the correct one. Even when it is, stakeholders will only support it under duress. Second, the stakeholder group loses all confidence in the leadership's ability to engage in a collaborative effort. Simply stated, power players may have temporarily resolved a problem, but by exerting power, they can create many new ones.

### The Divine Right of Kings

If it looks like a duck and quacks like a duck, it must be a moose. Remember *I'm the Boss and You're Not* from Chapter 1? This is where that person may reappear with a classic snatch-and-grab. The decision-making group are just vassals who are permitted to proffer possible solutions to the problem. When the appropriate group jousting has been done, it's time for the autocrat to take over. The solution is proclaimed by him or her. I have reviewed the options, and this is what we have decided. Any questions?

## Here Comes the Bulldozer

Power plays are not the exclusive right of kings. Subgroups, we will call them cabals, as well as controlling individuals, snatch and grab too. Rather than agreeing to and adhering to a preset criterion to choose a solution, these bulldozers choose their solution and plow over anyone who dares to disagree. This is a premeditated act. Getting together beforehand, they plot how to manipulate the group into submission. They threaten the weak, discredit the strong, and then bulldoze the solution through. Again, the solution may work, but this ramming process leaves a bad taste in everyone's mouth. It fractionates the group into winners and losers. The solution's implementation and sustainability are only owned by a few. This weakened state does not bode well.

## Two From Column One and One From Column Two...

This is the favored decision-making process of the utopian crowd. Rather than choosing a solution that best fits the criteria agreed to, they select a solution that makes people happy. Therefore, solutions are discarded based upon group members' personal distain. What remains is a neutered generality that is palpable to all. The solution chosen has little to do with the preset criteria. They then retreat to their work spaces and continue their normal routine, be it good, bad, or indifferent.

## The Spockeans

The *Spockeans* bury all emotions. You can see that this causes a pileup when arriving at a decision. Facts and logic are the only things that count when deciding on a solution. Spockeans consider human feelings weaknesses and detriments to quality decision-making. When feelings are expressed, they quickly discount them. They ignore those who are trying to point out the affective deficiencies of the solution. "Damn the torpedoes, full speed ahead." Alas, action is met with reaction; and the battle is on. Having no ability to empathize or sympathize, the *Spockeans* don't understand how things went wrong. Meanwhile, there is no solution to the problem: Decision-making processes are in disarray, and a whole set of problems has been created. Many *Spockean* decisions are the breeding places for crises. By the way, Ideologues are Spockeans with an attitude.

## Monkey See, Monkey Do

School politics can sometimes be overwhelmingly powerful. Go along to get along can become the sole criteria for choosing the solution. This is the "don't ruffle feathers" selection process. Small groups huddle; the message is sent via whispers and comments along the grapevine. Strategic complacency takes the place of participatory ownership as faculty and staff abrogate their responsibility and submit to the will of the powerful. Facades of cooperation and collaboration are painfully manufactured. It takes a great deal of psychic energy to maintain this ruse. At the end, faculty and staff quietly retreat to their offices and classrooms, keep their heads down, and endeavor to stay out of the limelight. Good sense goes underground. This fumble is becoming prevalent today, as powerful political ideologies hijack rational thinking when making decisions, and with that, choice and voice vanish.

## Putting It All Together: Weigh the Alternatives and Decide on a Solution

**Figure 7.1** Determining the Solution

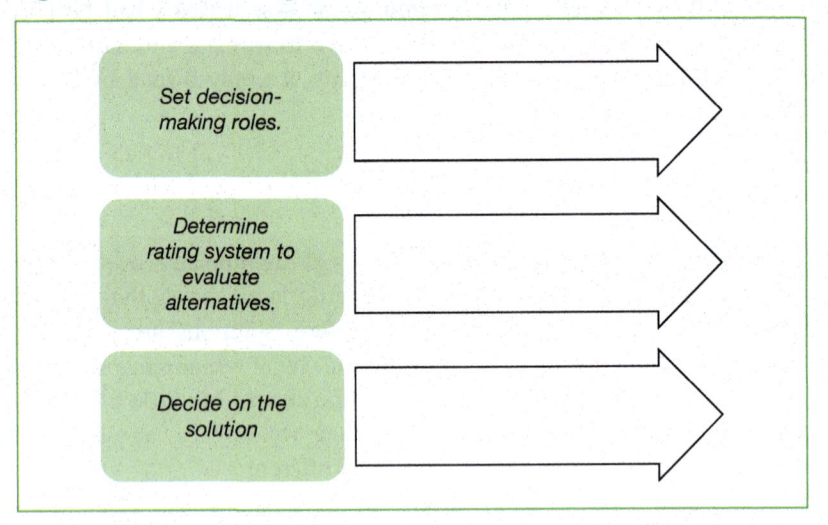

- Set decision-making roles.
- Determine rating system to evaluate alternatives.
- Decide on the solution

The potential for stepping into a fumble or a foible is very possible at this step. Clear and deliberate rules are the order of the day. Prior to entering any decision-making deliberation, the problem-solving group must clearly understand who is making the decision, and then determine the rules, rate possible solutions, and decide on the solution (see Figure 7.1). Taking the time to methodically pin down these three tasks will lay the foundation for a productive decision-making experience. Minimizing the importance of these tasks could be a fatal mistake.

## Task 1: Set Decision-Making Roles

▶ **Rule 13.** *Make sure the stakeholders know who is responsible for making decisions.*

## Theoretical Connections

For a more academic understanding of this concept, see Chapter 10, *Making Tough Decisions* (1990) by Paul Nutt.

When originally formed, the problem-solving group first identified the stakeholders. As part of that task, the group determined the level of involvement each stakeholder would have. Given stakeholder proximity, influence, and the nature of the problem, a stakeholder could be a decider, an advisor, or a participant. As with identifying the problem, the first task when making a decision is to reiterate stakeholder status and reaffirm their involvement in the decision-making process.

**Figure 7.2** Decision-Making Processes

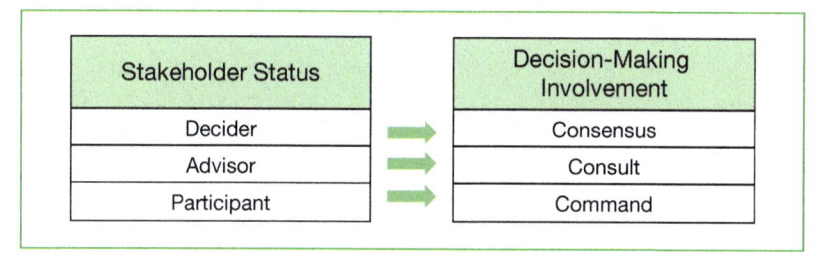

| Stakeholder Status | Decision-Making Involvement |
|---|---|
| Decider | Consensus |
| Advisor | Consult |
| Participant | Command |

As shown in the graphic (Figure 7.2), a stakeholder's involvement in decision-making varies based on status.

- Deciders have a direct say in the decision. They are the ones who evaluate solution options and make the final decision. They select the solution. Their involvement is consensual. Consensus here is defined as getting substantial agreement from the group. While the optimal outcome would be total agreement by the group, this is not always the case. When unanimity is not possible, consensus is attained by group members agreeing to support the decision. More will be said about this later.

- Advisers are consulted during the decision-making process. These stakeholders have knowledge, be it technical, political, or cultural, and can play a vital role in understanding and evaluating solution alternatives. Advisers provide information, being consulted either before or during the decision-making process. Consultation meetings can be one-on-one or group processes depending on the decision-making process.

- Participants are the stakeholders who must accept the decision and carry it out. Once the decision is made, they are commanded to implement it. The word command here can feel uncomfortable, and the term is used for exactly that reason. Whenever a decision is made that affects others without their input, this tends to automatically lead to resistance to that course of action. Consequently, deciders must take great care in assuring those affected by the decision will accept it. For every action there is a reaction. Careful preplanning and counting the votes can guarantee this reaction will be supportive. Giving a command is easy. Successfully carrying it out is another thing. Good leaders take great care in promoting positive follower involvement. As Peter Drucker mused, "A leader is one who has followers." A solution only works when the followers are willing carry it out.

In most cases, there will be stakeholders in all three categories. Their roles in the decision-making process should be clearly defined, and action plans detailing their involvement should be outlined. Being proactive here creates the first step in gaining stakeholder buy-in. Planning here also minimizes the possibilities of backtracking or retracting a decision. Be prepared for the possibilities.

## Task 2: Determine Rating System and Evaluate Alternatives

- *Rule 14.* Adhere to the processes and procedures agreed to for selecting a solution. Do not allow any deviations.

### Theoretical Connections

Tony Proctor's Chapter 10 in *Creative Problem-Solving of Managers* (2010) goes in-depth on this task. Chapter 4 in *The New Rational Manager* (1997) by Charles Kepner and Benjamin Tregoe, and Sandy Pokras's Part VIII in *Team Problem-Solving* also provide in-depth discussions on this topic.

The methods for evaluating solution options are varied and many. These assessment strategies range from the simple to the extremely complex. Processes such as decision trees, contingency analysis, similarity analysis, and multi-criteria analysis rely heavily on evaluative experience and statistical know-how. The business sector depends on these types of sophisticated algorithms and heuristics to make decisions. In the school world, such complexity is both impractical and for the most part, incomprehensible. Sticking to the basics, four evaluation systems are presented. These four can accommodate the assessment needs for most school decision-making. They are simple and efficient processes that are easily tallied and produce results that are clearly understandable to all. These four use the solution criteria as the foundation of their rating systems. They are Simple Counting; Counting 3, 2, 1; Weighted Ranking; and the Descriptive Rubric. A sample Solution Score Card (Figure 7.3). provides a template for listing criteria, rating performance, and tallying the results the three of numeric strategies. Descriptive Rubrics use a different format and are covered later.

**Figure 7.3** Criteria and Solution Documentation Sheet

### Solution Score Card

Solution:_____  Rank_____

| (1) Criterion Statement | (2) Descriptor | (3) Priority | (4) Standard | (5) Criterion Rating | (6) Tally |
|---|---|---|---|---|---|
|  | C = Component<br>A = Action<br>R = Result | M = Must<br>P = Prefer<br>N = Nice to | Indicant Statement | E = Exceeded<br>M = Met<br>P = Partially Met<br>N = Did Not Meet |  |
| **Criterion 1** |  |  |  |  |  |
|  |  |  |  |  |  |
|  |  |  |  |  |  |
|  |  |  |  |  |  |
| **Criterion N** |  |  |  |  |  |

**Total Score_____**

Here is how the Solution Score Card works. Columns 1 through 4 record the criterion information developed earlier by the problem-solving group. Column 1 is a succinct description of the criterion. Column 2 identifies the criterion type. Column 3 lists priority. Column 4 is the performance standard. Column 5 rates the solution option's performance for each criterion standard using a range from *exceeding standards* to *not meeting standard*. Column 5 documents the results for the solution-rating process. Once the performance evaluation is completed for each option, the options are ranked according to their best fit to the problem and recorded in Column 6.

*Task. Evaluate the Solution Options.*
Evaluating solution options is a three-step process: (1) Assess each option's success at meeting criteria standards; (2) compare the performance of each solution option using one of the four evaluation strategies; and (3) select the best option based on the results of the evaluation.

▶ Rate solution options by criteria standards.

Before an evaluation of the solution options can be done, the results of the criteria assessment must be tabulated and scored. Gathering the results of the solution search, one or more members of the problem-solving team can organize the findings and produce a description of each solution option. Applying the solution criteria standards developed earlier, the members score each option, based on adherence to the standard using one of the four evaluation systems. The results are then documented. The Solution Score Card can be used to document the numeric evaluation systems.

▶ Compare performance using one of the four solution assessment strategies.

**Figure 7.4** Documenting a Solution Criteria Performance (Simple Counting)

## Solution Score Card

Solution:_____  Rank_____

| (1) Criterion Statement | (2) Descriptor | (3) Priority | (4) Standard | (5) Criterion Rating | (6) Tally |
|---|---|---|---|---|---|
| | C = Component<br>A = Action<br>R = Result | M = Must<br>P = Prefer<br>N = Nice to | Indicant Statement | E = Exceeded<br>M = Met<br>P = Partially Met<br>N = Did Not Meet | |
| Budget reduction of 5% | R | M | Operations budget reduced by $250,000 | E | |
| Personnel allocations remain at current year levels | R | M | Personnel costs reflect present staffing adjusted for salary and non salary cost increases predicted for upcoming year. | M | |

Total Score _____

- *Simple Counting*

   As depicted in Figure 7.4, this strategy determines whether the solution option has exceeded (E), met (M), partially met (P), or (N) failed to meet criteria standards. Once all criteria have been assessed, the Es, Ms, Ps, and the Ns are counted. The solution option scoring the best combination becomes the preferred choice (Figure 7.5).

**Figure 7.5** Documenting a Solution Criteria Performance (3,2,1)

## Solution Score Card

Solution:_____    Rank_____

| (1) Criterion Statement | (2) Descriptor | (3) Priority | (4) Standard | (5) Criterion Rating | (6) Tally |
|---|---|---|---|---|---|
|  | C = Component<br>A = Action<br>R = Result | M = Must<br>P = Prefer<br>N = Nice to | Indicant Statement | Must = 3<br>Prefer = 2<br>Nice to = 1<br>Did Not Meet = 0 |  |
| Criterion 1 |  | M |  | 3 | 3 |
| Criterion 2 |  | N |  | 1 | 1 |

Total Score _____ 4 __

- *Counting 3, 2, 1*

   This simple strategy assigns value based on the priority designation of the criterion. A *Must* having the greatest priority is assigned a *3*; a *Preference* is assigned a value of *2*, and a *Nice to* is assigned a *1*. Solution options that meet criterion standards are given the numerical rating corresponding to their priority. Once all criteria have been assessed and rated, the scores are tallied and totaled. The solution option scoring the highest number of points is selected as the optimum choice.

**Figure 7.6** Documenting a Solution Criteria Performance (Weighted Ranking)

### Solution Score Card

Solution:_____    Rank_____

| (1) Criterion Statement | (2) Descriptor | (3) Priority | (4) Standard | (5) Criterion Rating | (6) Tally |
|---|---|---|---|---|---|
| | C = Component<br>A = Action<br>R = Result | 3 = Must<br>2 = Prefer<br>1 = Nice to | Indicant Statement | 3 = Exceeded<br>2 = Met<br>1 = Partially Met<br>0 = Did Not Meet | Col 3 × Col 5<br>=<br>Tally |
| Criterion 1 | | 3 | | 2 | 6 |
| Criterion 2 | | 1 | | 3 | 3 |

Total Score_____9___

- *Weighted Ranking*

    This strategy assigns differing values to priorities and performance. As can be seen in Figure 7.6, a *Must* priority is given the greatest value 3, while a *Nice to* is given the least value 1. The ranking of standards is treated the same way. *Exceeding Standards* is rated a 3, while *Meeting Standards* is given a 2, and so on. Once each criterion has been rated by priority for performance, the scores from Columns 3 and 5 are multiplied to provide a composite tally score for that criterion. When all criteria have been rated, the composite scores are summed to provide a total score for the solution option. The option with the highest composite score becomes the solution choice.

    The problem-solving group can choose to vary the use of this strategy. Criterion could each be assigned individual values or the type of criterion (*Component, Action, and Result*) could be assigned particular values as well.

- *Descriptive Rubric*

"Not everything that can be counted counts, and not everything that counts can be counted." William Bruce Cameron said it succinctly. There are certain problems where their solution options cannot be accurately assessed using a numeric rating system (Figure 7.7).

**Figure 7.7** Documenting a Solution Criteria Performance (Descriptive Rubric), an Example

| Element | Meets Standards | Partially Meets Standards | Does Not Meet Standards |
|---|---|---|---|
| **Identify the elements of the problem.** | A well delineated problem description accurately depicts the who, what, when, where, and why or how of the situation. A concise and understandable problem statement presents the most salient accountings of the members reporting, and is understood by the group. | A partial or general description of the problem has been developed by the group. The problem is not clearly understood by all. The problem description can be interpreted in more than one way. | The situation needing attention has not been described. The who, what, when, where and, why of the problem is not understood. Members have a different view of the problem, and are proceeding to try to solve it. |
| **Determine the type of problem.** | The group has a common understanding of the impact of the situation. It has been able to determine whether the problem is a deficit deficiency, emerging opportunity, sequential improvement, or new undertaking. The group has a sense of how to respond solve the problem and understands the power of the problem. | Some members of the group have an understanding of the impact of the situation. The group is not of one mind as to the type of problem the situation represents. The group does not have a clear sense how to respond to solve the problem. | The group has no understanding of the impact of the situation. It does not understand whether the problem presented represents a deficit deficiency, emerging opportunity, sequential improvement, or new undertaking for the school, and therefore has no understanding of how to solve the problem. |
| **Determine the level of difficulty the problem poses.** | The group clearly recognizes what they know when don't know about the problem. They have determined whether the problem is a simple, complicated, complex, or chaotic situation, and understand the type of knowledge needed to fully define and solve the problem. | There is some understanding of what the group knows about the problem. Some members have determined the level of difficulty the problem poses, while others are not in agreement. The group has a partial understanding of the type of knowledge necessary to define and solve the problem. | The group has no understanding of the level of difficulty the problem poses. It has not identified whether the problem is simple, complicated, complex or chaotic. It does not have an understanding of the top and knowledge necessary to solve the problem and fully define it. |
| **Determine the urgency to solve the problem.** | The group is clear that the problem's impact and the school's ability to address it. The problem has clearly been evaluated based on the opportunity or threat that it poses and the strengths or weaknesses of the school to address it. The group has a clear understanding of the problem's urgency. | There's a partial understanding of the problem's impact by some group members. Problem has been partially evaluated, but not completely understood as an opportunity or threat be imposed on the school. The group is not determined the school's capability to respond. | There is no clear understanding of the program's impact on the school, and the school's ability to address it. Though evaluation of the problem has been conducted to determine whether the problem represents an opportunity or threat, and the strengths and weaknesses of the school to respond. |

While the three quantitative strategies can be used to score or rank criteria performance, the rubric uses written language to describe criteria attainment. There are three advantages for using a descriptive rubric. Descriptive rubrics

- Provide better assessment tools for evaluating performance problems and problems in the affective domain.
- Provide transparent and clear assessment measures that can be easily understood by stakeholders.
- Can be used summatively to judge criteria attainment as well as formatively to be used as indicators for solution improvement.

Here is how they work. As shown in Figure 7.7, the elements that make up the parts of the solution are listed in the far-left column. The levels of attainment for meeting the standard required are listed in the top row. The *Level of Attainment* categories in the example are the following: *Meets Standards, Partially Meets Standards, Does Not Meet Standards*. If required, levels of attainment can be broken down further to four or five categories. A concise statement describing the condition or performance for each level of attainment is written for each element and distributed accordingly on the grid. The completed table is used as an evaluation sheet to rate how each solution option performs. Rubric descriptors can be constructed in two ways:

- Group members having content expertise develop the rubric descriptors, or outside experts are used. Once the draft of the descriptors is completed, the stakeholder group reviews the document and agrees with its contents.
- Using an inductive process, group members brainstorm the parts of each descriptor creating descriptors for each level of attainment. The final draft of the descriptor grid is agreed to by the group.

Before the rubric can be used to rate solution options, group members assigned to that task must calibrate their use of the rubric to ensure each rater would be assigning the same scores to solution options. The calibration of member observations is accomplished through an interrater process. Together, raters review one or more practice solution options and compare their scores. Where differences occur, those differences are discussed and appropriate adjustments are made. This process is repeated until the group is satisfied they are rating in unison.

Once the interrater process has been completed, pairs of members rate each solution options in the blind. Where a rating differs, a third member adjudicates. This process is continued until all solution options have been evaluated. The options are then ranked according to their performance to standards, the highest score becoming the preferred option.

Before leaving this strategy, it should be noted that rubric development can be a time-consuming process. However, where a problem solution requires descriptive assessment to be accurately evaluated, there is no choice. It is recommended that descriptive rubrics be constructed when developing solution criteria.

▶ Select the best option.

Using one of the four strategies for evaluating solution options makes selecting the preferred option an easy task. In most cases, the preferred solution will clearly surface through the ranking process. Where this isn't the case, the total group discusses the results, offering the pros and cons of the contenders, until the best contender is chosen by the group.

## TASK CUE CARD

- *Desired Outcome:* The Preferred Solution to the Problem is Selected.

- *Group Organizers: Solution Score Card; Simple Counting, Counting 3,2,1, Weighted Ranking* or *Descriptive Rubric; Spend-a-Dot; Round Robin; Thumbs Up*

- *Your Team Lesson Plan:* Begin with an organization session. Post the Solution Scorecard and the four solution assessment strategies on flipcharts in full view of the group. First, review the Solution Scorecard. Make sure that all group members fully understand how to use the card. Then review each of the solution assessment strategies and discuss the advantages and disadvantages of each one. Have the group select a solution assessment strategy using Spend-a-Dot process. After compiling the results, do a Thumbs Up process to ensure all members will be comfortable with the strategy chosen.

- Depending on the nature, power, and potency of the problem, either a select subcommittee of the members or the membership of the whole group can assess and weigh each solution option according to the rules of the assessment strategy. In certain situations, the use of subgroups to triangulate results can be used as well.

- Once the solution assessments are completed and a preferred option is selected, have the group gathered in toto to review results. Where triangulation was used, ensure there is common agreement on the selection of the preferred option by all groups. Quickly review the findings from the assessment process. Provide time for the group members to ask questions and seek clarification. Once a common understanding of the process is completed, do a Thumbs-Up, Thumbs-Down process to determine the group's acceptance of the solution for action. When unanimity is not present, members work to adjust the solution, until all deciders can agree.

- Estimated time will vary depending on the rating strategy chosen.

## Task 3: Decide on the Solution

Wasn't a solution chosen in the previous step? The short answer is yes. The last step in Task 2 had the group select the preferred alternative. However, one more discussion remains. **This is the most critical point in the problem-solving process**. A solution has finally been proffered that the stakeholder group agreed to. As we discussed earlier when considering defining a problem, there is a good chance individual group members are interpreting the meaning of the solution in different ways. Also, while members rationally agreed to the solution, they might not be emotionally ready to follow through to carry out the solution.

> *Rule 16. Stakeholder deciders must come to consensus on implementing the have attempted to write the Foibles and alternative selected.*

### Theoretical Connections

For a thorough discussion on this topic, see Sam Kaner, *Facilitator's Guide to Participatory Decision-Making, Part 5* (2014).

Consensus does not mean unanimity. Coming to consensus means the group has a common agreement or accord to go forward with the matter under discussion. This does not mean that every member is fully in agreement with every aspect of the solution. It means that individuals are comfortable enough to see the solution go forward and to support it. Begin the consensus process by doing a round robin with the group, having each member reflect on their understanding of what the solution entails. Once completed, each member has to provide input to clear up any misunderstandings. Now, record the final solution statement on a flipchart. Read the final statement aloud and then poll the group for agreement. Members can respond in one of three ways:

- Agreeing to support the solution
- Agreeing to allow the solution to go forward without personal resistance
- Disagreeing to support the solution at this time

If the polling of the group results in members voting to agree or not resist the solution going forward, then a consensus has been reached. If a large percentage of the group has voted to allow the solution go forward without resistance rather than agreeing with the solution, further review and adjustments of the solution may be in order. When one or more members disagrees about supporting the solution, then further discussion about the solution must take place. The guiding question for this discussion is addressed to the individuals not supporting the solution. The question is "What changes in the solution need to occur for you to either let the solution go forward without resistance or support the solution?" The group works with the individual until a common agreement can be made as to the changes in the solution so individuals not in support will join the rest of the group in consensus.

There may be a few times when this process will not result in total agreement. When this occurs, leadership must decide on the course of action based upon the power and potency of the problem and the significance of the stakeholder or holders in resisting moving the solution forward. If the problem-solving process as discussed in this text is adhered to, the chances for negative response to the solution are extremely slight. However, if fumbles and foibles are part of the decision-making process, then stakeholder resistance is a possibility, and it's a probability if these fumbles and foibles significantly damaged group voice and choice.

Once consensus has been reached, it's time to celebrate. In many cases, this problem-solving process has been a long and arduous one. Stakeholders have dedicated their time and talent into trying to resolve the problem and should be congratulated for their efforts. It's time for applause.

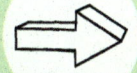

## Consider This...

Tired? Good, that means careful thought and action have been used. Practice may not make perfect as every problem has its own personality, but using this system for problem solving will become easier and, eventually, second nature. Encouraging voice and choice among stakeholders will also lessen future problems as the staff becomes more aware of issues that show up as possible future problems. Nipping a problem in the bud is always better than having it become a major explosion.

**CHAPTER 8**

# Solve the Problem

> Many people don't focus enough on execution. If you make a commitment to get something done, you need to follow through on that commitment.
>
> —Kenneth I. Chenault

The Yogi said it best when commenting on the Mets' chances against the Reds in the 1973 National League Pennant race, "It ain't over 'til it's over." Knowing what to do is one thing; knowing how to do it is another. While the solution has been determined, the problem has not been solved. The "what" of the solution only provides half of the answer. How the solution is carried out is the other half, and it is the "how" that solves the problem. The final step in the problem-solving process plans and guides the "how," the path to successfully implement the solution. Four tasks are undertaken by leadership here.

1. A workable action plan is built to carry out the solution.
2. An evaluation plan is developed to assess and correct solution implementation and to judge solution effectiveness.
3. Resources are assigned as needed to successfully complete the task.
4. Management strategies are calendared to include progress reports and assessment reviews to monitor and guide solution implementation.

Putting the solution into action means staff engagement, resource appropriation, job assignment, goal setting, and the list goes on. Deciding on a solution is a starting point but not the finish line for solving the problem. The leadership and the problem-solving group now must shift their attention from what to do to how to do it. Serious follow-through is essential. All too often, the solution is agreed to, and the problem solvers pat each other on the back and walk away, leaving the implementation of the solution firmly stuck in midair. Decision implementation is assumed. Putting the solution into effect should not be left to happenstance or interpretation.

The stakeholders, who methodically came to the solution decision, are the best qualified and best served when they have a hand in planning the implementation. That's not enough. Remember the Burns' poem: "The best laid plans of mice and men gang aft agley." Things never go according to plan, so plans need to be adjusted and staff needs to adapt. Sound evaluation strategies proactively guide implementation adjustments and need to be set in motion at this critical juncture. Think about how often school problem-solving groups consider evaluation plans for solution implementation or for that matter, actually evaluate the success of the initiatives they set in motion. Many times, program and policy decisions are determined, but they are wistfully spirited into space never to be heard of again. When the "how" is not attended to, the "what" is up for grabs. Since this is the case, why bother trying to solve the problem in a rational way in the first place? The last stage of the problem-solving process is probably more important than the first. In far too many instances, this is what happens instead.

## Foibles and Fumbles When Solving the Problem

### Ain't in My Vocabulary

For this group, the follow-up for implementing a solution is not their problem. They have more important things to do. Implementation planning is just another form of administrivia, and they are not into that kind of thing. Besides, such tasks are beneath them. Their job was to grace the group with their superior intelligence and astute reasoning. Get their hands dirty? Not on your life. Whether it works or not is not their thing, nor should it be. On to the pressing things in life. Pass the tea and crumpets.

### Leave It to Beaver

The *Let Mikey Do It* crowd from Chapter 5 are alive and well. This group will do anything to pass the buck. Formal job descriptions were not important until now, when the solution of the problem has been determined. This is the moment they decide to invoke those hallowed words, "It's not in my job description," casually saunter away, and toss the implementation of the solution like a hot potato into someone else's lap.

Or as we saw in Chapter 5, they can execute their favorite "go to" move—the departmental sidestep. The long-revered sidestep has a broad range of targets. It could be the English department again! They are a favorite prey for high school faculties. Maybe it is the third-grade teachers this time. They seem to be the brain trust "go to" for elementary schools. College faculties just form committees, where most solutions go to die. The all-time favorites, however, are the HR and business departments. They'll create the official dictum to make the "boo-boo" go away. The great thing about *Leaving It to Beaver* is the folks don't have to get involved in the boring efforts of making something happen, and they can always say "I told you so" if the solution doesn't work.

## We'll Take It From Here

It feels like being in a Douglas Adams movie where someone shouts out the phrase "So long, and thanks for the fish." Those power group devils are back at it. If they play their cards right, they have their final chance to take control. Here's their script. Now that the solution has been figured out, the stakeholder group isn't needed any more. So they, the power folks, will take it from here. Under the guise of either administrative responsibility or the mantle of senior experience and expertise, they pull off the old "snatch and grab." Wielding their power of authority or expertise, they yank the solution implementation from the group, dismiss the stakeholders, adjourn the meeting, and take over. It may have taken awhile, but these folks are persistent. They're back in the saddle again, and by way, "Thanks for the fish, you all."

## Get 'er Done

Herb Simon coined the term *satisficing* in 1956. It means rather than taking the extra time necessary to perfect the solution, create the simplest approach that will meet acceptable solution standards. Well, this is not what we mean here. "Dotting Is and crossing Ts, we're really not doing that." We want to wrap this thing up and get on with it. So we know what we have to do; let's just go out and do it. With "A fiery horse, a cloud of dust, and a hearty 'Hi-yo, Silver!'" They are off like the Lone Ranger. Most times this cowboy strategy plays out like another manifestation of adolescent bravado or the running of the bulls in Pamplona.

### An Epilogue

> To make no mistakes is not in the power of man; but from their errors and mistakes the wise and good learn wisdom for the future.
>
> —Plutarch

We, the authors, have attempted to write the Foibles and Fumbles to get your attention. The vignettes were not meant to demean or shame those, who for the most part, are trying their best to help others. The vignettes chosen from the myriad of examples available are the ones that stood out. They are the ones that still make us still feel guilty, angry, or embarrassed. They are the ones school staffs keep doing over and over and seldom, if ever, lead to good decision-making or successful solutions. They do, however, lead to poor interpersonal relations, low morale, and low productivity. Because of their toxicity, they are great examples of what not to do. Please, take it from us, they are not good ideas.

Some vignettes used sarcasm and humor and were meant to innocently poke fun at ourselves and others, so hopefully, with a chuckle, you, the reader, would say, "Okay that's funny, and that's something I am not doing."

There were some vignettes framing realities that simply could not muster humor. Their realities are so emotionally debilitating, they can't be framed in a light-hearted manner. This was particularly the case when dealing with real authoritarians.

One can't be light-hearted when addressing situations where leadership makes it a practice to bully, subjugate, and control. Where, as Gareth Morgan so aptly put it, people are relegated to a "psychic prison." While these occasions are particularly damaging in business, they are devastating in education, and there is no humor in that.

As Plutarch, the noted Greek philosopher/historian advised, while we all make mistakes, our Foibles and Fumbles, we should be wise and learn from them. Hopefully, you, the reader, have learned something from ours. As Otto von Bismarck said, "Only a fool learns from his own mistakes. The wise man learns from the mistakes of others."

## Putting It All Together: Solve the Problem

> Talk doesn't cook rice.
>
> — Chinese Proverb

**Figure 8.1** Solving the Problem

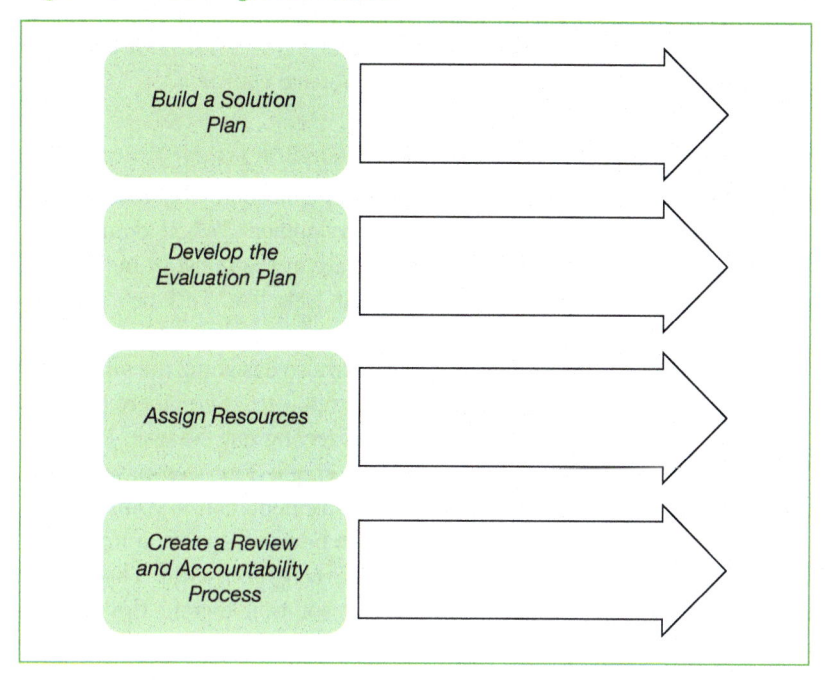

- Build a Solution Plan
- Develop the Evaluation Plan
- Assign Resources
- Create a Review and Accountability Process

Finding a solution is like reaching the climax of a movie or a play. It is the decisive moment of the problem-solving process. Indeed, all things have come together. There is resolution. However, the most important part of the drama is yet to come—the denouement—where the matters of how the solution is to be accomplished are laid out. Naming a solution does not solve the problem. Taking action to realize the solution does (see Figure 8.1). The stakeholder group's job isn't done until concrete actions are taken to set the solution in motion and manage its implementation to reach the goal intended.

> **Rule 17.** *This is no time for a pat on the back. Shift your mental gears; get ahead of the group, and complete the follow-through procedure for the implementation of the solution.*

It may seem subtle, but a huge shift in thinking happens when solving the problem. Up until now, the thinking about the problem and its solution has been in the abstract. Now concrete thinking takes over to actualize the solution; the group's work moves from thought to practice.

This means a shift where the group's concrete sequential thinkers assume primacy from the abstract random folks. No longer a free-wheeling give and take, the conversation now turns methodical and granular. The feeling tone moves from tense and exciting to dull and mundane. This cerebral power shift comes at a time when most of the group is ready to call it a day. Being oblivious to this change will surely seed cognitive dissonance in the group and set the group up to Foible and Fumble.

> ***Rule 18.*** *It's time for a timeout. Let the group take a deep breath and regenerate. Perhaps celebrate. Retool and restart the group again. It has a new purpose and mission. So meeting roles, structures, and norms need to be reviewed to meet the new charge.*

## Set the Stage for a Solution: Use PAAR

Solving a problem is like doing many things in education—like lesson planning, schedule building, and curriculum development. When doing these things, staff is flying the airplane while they are in the midst of building it. Most experienced educators know what that feels like. This ball juggling becomes even more complicated when setting out to implement the solution.

When implementing a solution, the staff is also designing the aircraft, in addition to flying while building it. Sounds complicated. Sure, there are a lot of moving parts, but here's a simple way of carrying out the task. PAAR it. PAAR (plan, assign, assess, and review) is a simple four-step process that allows stakeholders to actively manage the implementation to completion.

Solution oversight and development can be conducted in a myriad of ways, ranging from direct participation to receiving reports. The nature of the problem and the particulars of the solution dictate the type of stakeholder involvement. Typically, leadership, or a subgroup of the stakeholders, are designated to the PAAR task.

The timeframe for carrying out the tasks for solving the problem varies as well. Simple solutions can be carried out in a matter of minutes. Some complex or chaotic solutions may stretch over long timeframes and require many PAAR work sessions. Again, it depends on the nature of the problem and the elements of the solution.

Regardless of the composition of the team or the timeframe for the work, focus and follow-through are the two key ingredients for successfully bringing the solution to fruition, and PARR ensures they are in place. Here are the PAAR particulars (Figure 8.2).

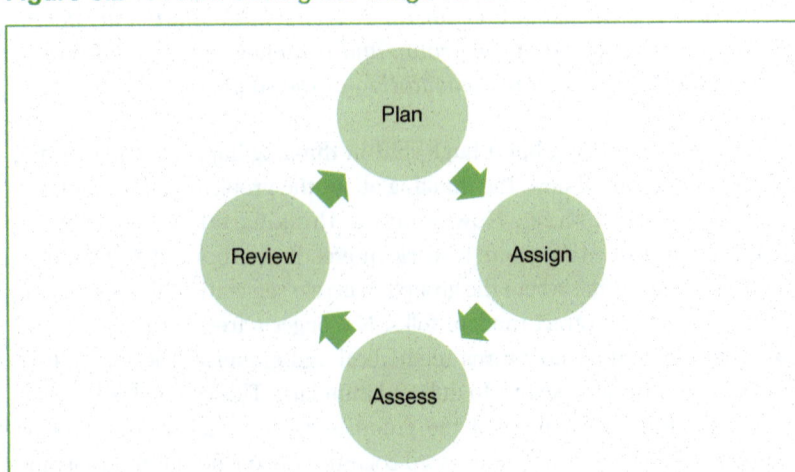

**Figure 8.2** PAAR: Setting the Stage for Success

# Task 1: Plan the Solution

Solving the problem begins with a plan. As old Yogi said, "If you don't know where you are going, you'll end up someplace else." Solutions look simpler to accomplish when they are still figments of the mind. When thought moves to action, the unexpected tends to show up. Those gnarly details present themselves when figuring out how to do it. Successfully handling the gnarly details is a secret to succeeding.

Planning creates solutions to the "gnarlies," while putting the 5Ws in place to realize the intended end. Most importantly, planning provides the way of thinking, a mindset for focusing on solution implementation in real-time. Most plans do not go the way they are planned. However, the creative and reflective mindset established by the planning process creates a mental agility that is ideally suited to seeing shortcomings, wrong ways, and false starts and then adapting to them. The solution plan accomplishes three functions; planning, organizing, and timing. The graphic presented in Figure 8.3 depicts the elements of a solution plan.

**Figure 8.3** The Solution Plan

| Action to Be Completed | Key People Involved | Lead Person | Resources Required | Expected Outcome | Anticipated Time frame | When Completed |
|---|---|---|---|---|---|---|
| | | | | | | |

The typical solution plan is a written strategy listing the who, what, where, when, why, and how the solution is to be accomplished. The actions are chronicled into a timeline that outlines the work from start to finish. The solution plan identifies the personnel tasked to do the work and the leadership responsible for managing the plan. It specifies the resources (i.e., finances, materials, spaces, and other assets) necessary to effectively carry out the work. Specific intermediate and terminal outcomes, originating from the solution criteria, are listed along the action task line. Benchmarks of progress and completion are also placed in the critical phases of the plan. Each entry is placed along a timeline noting a beginning and a completion date.

The solution plan tells the story of the solution's travels from thought to reality. Make it as useful as possible. It is not a litany of disconnected activities but a sequence of connected actions that, when followed, logically construct the solution. It is the outline for action. Include the necessary pertinent elements, but do not go overboard. The plan is the blueprint and not the house. Here is a rule: The plan must be comprehensive enough that a person independently reviewing it can mirror the work that is actually being done. It should also be succinct and concise enough that any stakeholder can easily follow along and understand the strategy and its outcomes. Figure 8.4 is a simple checklist of to-dos when building a solution plan.

**Figure 8.4** Solution Plan To-Do Checklist

| | |
|---|---|
| **Organize:** | Set objectives and outcomes. |
| | Develop a specific course of action. |
| | Identify tasks. |
| | Set priorities and sequence of events. |
| | Assign responsibilities. |
| | Establish milestones and benchmarks. |
| **Procure Resources:** | People. |
| | Materials and supplies. |
| | Facilities. |
| | Operating budget. |
| **Set Timetable:** | Include slack time. |
| | Include gap time. |
| | Set in real time. |
| | Allow extra time. |

## Task 2: Assign Resources

This seems a pretty straight forward task. Just ask for volunteers, gather them together, and get on with it. While solving a problem needs a good plan, a constructive monitoring of progress, and revision as needed, it most importantly requires the right people to make it happen. As Jim Collins said, "Get the right people on the bus, the wrong people off the bus, and the right people in the right seats." Take the same care in selecting the lead person and key personnel for solving the problem, as was done in selecting members of the stakeholder group when taking on the problem.

Creating and maintaining are two different tasks requiring two different skillsets. Maintenance keeps things working. It preserves what is already in existence. Creation, on the other hand, is the production of things from midair. Creators make a real thing from an idea. Getting the "right people on the bus" means choosing leadership and an implementation team who are creators, not maintainers.

It should almost go without saying that those selected need to be committed to the solution and be willing to work hard to make it happen. Additionally, due to the creative nature of solution implementation, those selected should have creative dispositions.

Look for leaders and team members who have balanced personalities; individuals who are inquisitive and aren't afraid to try something new and, most importantly, people who are adaptable. The creative individual has a specific work profile as well. He or she is deliberate when tasking and isn't afraid to build things from scratch. They are quick to know when something isn't working and also being quick to discard it and start over. Above all, this individual is a team player who will work collegially to create the solution.

Finally, the creative staff member is a reflective thinker. This person is constantly looking at what is being done and realistically evaluating the work to ensure it is accomplishing what is required.

Assigning is not just about getting the right people on the bus but also for making sure they have the necessary resources to complete their mission. This is not the time for amateurs. Bring on the quartermasters. In the military, a quartermaster is the officer responsible for providing quarters, rations, clothing, and other supplies. In the school context, these are the expert staff responsible for finances, facilities, curriculum, instruction, and others who can accurately determine and budget for the necessary resources to bring the solution plan to realization. Bring in the experts as necessary to review the solution plan and make considered resource recommendations.

## Task 3: Create an Assessment Process

A comprehensive evaluation design is a two-pronged effort. It is summative. It judges whether a desired outcome has been reached. It is also formative. It assesses progress and provides constructive feedback to help the team adjust resources and work to reach the intended goal.

### Formative Evaluation

A good formative evaluation uncovers design defects and implementation deficiencies. It creates the adjustments necessary to provide the staff a better plane, as they are flying it. A good formative evaluation is an insurance policy protecting against solution failure. It is commonly understood that the bricks and mortar of real life never exactly turn out as designed on paper. New realizations occur; events actually happen in real-time. The gnarly "should be's" show up. The curriculum should really look like this. Or we should be teaching using this strategy instead. The nasty thing about gnarly "should bes" is they don't clearly show themselves unless they are searched for and, if they are left undetected, can turn into gremlins and crash the airplane.

Formative evaluation is really action learning. Remember, this process was created by Reg Revan and was introduced back in Chapter 5 as a preferred problem-solving procedure for simple problems. Action learning is also an ideal process to use for assessing the success of solution implementation. It is a metacognitive process the staff can use to direct their efforts forward, reaching the intended solution. Here is how it works.

**Figure 8.5** The Formative Evaluation Process

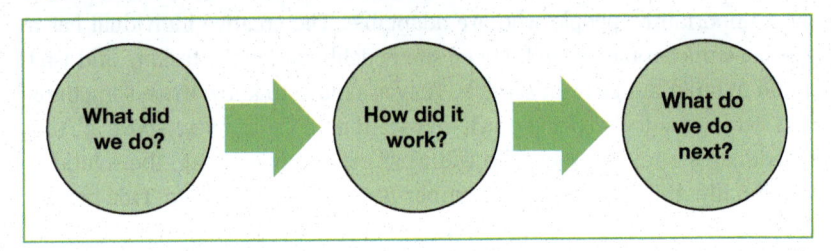

What did we do? → How did it work? → What do we do next?

As depicted in Figure 8.5, three simple questions drive the formative assessment. What did we do? How did it work? What do we do next? On closer inspection, one can see these questions drive a *discrepancy analysis* (what is; what should be; what is the difference). When conducting a formative assessment episode, the staff:

1. Observes the performance of 5Ws of the targeted elements of the Solution Plan. These observations can be done chronologically, by benchmark, or by a specific topic. Detailed descriptions are formulated that provide an accurate accounting that answers the question, "*What did we do?*"

2. Reviews the *actions to be completed* and *outcomes* statements contained in the Solution Plan (see Figure 8.3) for the elements being assessed to answer the question, "*What should be?*" Now, the descriptions of "what is" and the statements of "what should be" are examined side-by-side to determine what deficiencies or discrepancies are present, (the gnarlies).

3. Develops strategies and tactics to remediate any deficiencies or discrepancies found, revising the plans and actions being conducted to answer the question, "*What do we do next?*" Course corrections are made to steer the work toward a successful conclusion.

The frequency and depth of formative assessments is dependent on the staff's present knowledge about the inner-workings of the solution. Experience has shown the more frequent the assessment, the quicker the intended outcomes are realized.

Figure 8.6  An Evaluation Template

| Action | Key People Involved | Lead Person | Resources Used | Outcome | Time Frame | Date Completed | Assessment | | | Notes |
|---|---|---|---|---|---|---|---|---|---|---|
| | | | | | | | Meets | Partially Meets | Does Not Meet | |
| | | | | | | | | | | |

## Summative Evaluation

The problem-solving process is really not fully completed until the problem has been solved. The final task in the process is the production and review of the report card on the solution. Serious time, talent, and resources have been given to the problem-solving process and the development and execution of the preferred solution. It's time to ask two questions: *Did it work?* and *Was it worth it?*

Once the solution implementation is completed, a final assessment is made to judge the success of the effort. The specific elements listed in the solution criteria and performance outcomes detailed in the Solution Plan are compared to actual performance and results. According to the standards set, the outcomes are judged to have either met or failed to meet standards. Grades are given. If the solution passed, it's on to the next thing. If the solution failed, then it is back to the drawing board and a new action learning episode. Experience has taught us that all too often, the road to success is built on many failures. Persistence usually pays off. As Thomas Edison said, "I have not failed, I've just found 10,000 ways that won't work."

Figure 8.6 depicts a template that can be used to record the Solution Plan and both the results of summative and formative assessments. Documents, such as this example, have multiple uses, historical records, communication devices, and advanced organizers. This or some other design should be used when conducting a PAAR.

A side note about half-lives. Nothing works forever. A common fact seems to hold true about schools. Solutions are not just implemented, they are sown into the school's very fabric, cemented into the school operational structure. While initially resolving problems, these initiatives can continue to exist ad infinitum because *that's the way things are done around here*. Programs and processes created as solutions have end dates. It is not very often school leadership or school staffs check the expiration dates on their systems. Perhaps they should.

## Task 4: Review Progress

Getting people on the same page and developing a common understanding is an essential prerequisite for good problem solving. Good solution follow-through requires the same thing. People must stay on the same page and be of common mind until the solution has proven itself. The stakeholders, whether they are deciders, advisors, or participants, play vital roles in the monitoring and guiding of solution implementation. Their involvement in shepherding the implementation through not only provides feedback from various vantage points but also engenders confidence in the process and the leadership. Constructive involvement here also promotes a stronger commitment to sustaining the effort. Paying attention to keeping the stakeholders in the loop during implementation will pay off many times over. Remember, inclusion engenders trust and respect. Trust and respect build teams, and teams get things done. So what does a standard review process look like?

**Figure 8.7** Progress Loops

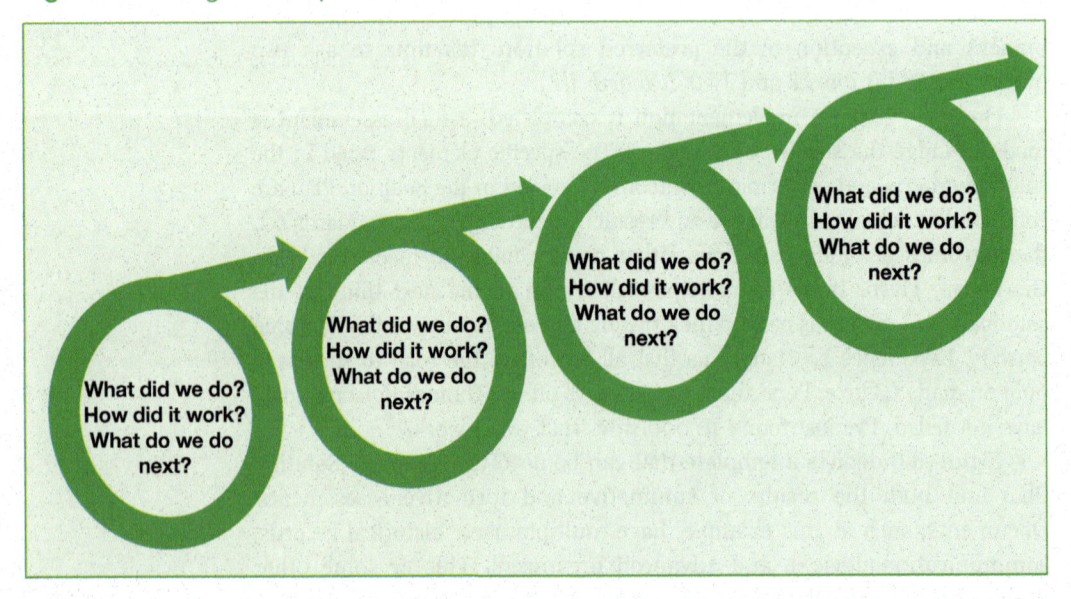

The review process is a series of observations and analyses that lead to a discrepancy analysis on the progress of solution implementation. As depicted in Figure 8.7, each episode assesses what is being done, whether it is meeting the standards of the criteria set, and if not, the appropriate course of action to take to make remediation adjustments. Let's call each episode a progress loop. Each loop provides the baseline for the next loop. Chris Argyris called them learning loops, and they are the bread and butter of learning organizations and continuous improvement. Progress loop reviews can be scheduled on a chronological basis, scheduled in conjunction with action or task completion or according to pre-determined benchmarks in the solution plan.

> **Rule 19.** *Solution reviews are strategically carried out during solution implementation.*

Solution reviews are not casual afterthoughts or events to be held once the implementation has been completed. They are meant to be used as communication and decision-making vehicles to keep stakeholders apprised and involved. Not paying attention here can lead to program drift or worse.

## The Elements of a Review Meeting

Typical review meetings are divided into three sections: a presentation of work to date, an assessment of performance, and a strategy and tactics section:

1. Work presentation. Referencing the action statements contained in the *Evaluation Report* as a basis for discussion, the implementation team presents a status report on the work being completed and accomplished during the time period designated by the review. This status report should be distributed to the stakeholder group for study prior to the meeting date. As necessary a question-and-answer session follows the report, providing further explanation and clarification of the work.

2. Performance review. The outcome and assessment statements contained in the evaluation report are measured against the actions completed to chart progress. First, a formative assessment is presented discussing performance and analyzing any discrepancies uncovered. Any deficiencies are clearly noted. Where appropriate, final completion outcomes are reviewed. Where criteria or standards were not met, deficiencies are clearly noted.

3. Next steps. Where deficiencies and discrepancies are noted, strategies and tactics are presented and discussed. A best course of action is determined to ameliorate the problem. In most

cases, the implementation team or a stakeholder subgroup prepares these recommendations beforehand. Their recommendations are then used as the basis for discussion. Review sessions continue until solution implementation has been completed. If done correctly, the final summative evaluation on solution implementation should find all outcomes have been successfully attained. Good formative guidance guarantees good summative outcomes.

## Theoretical Connections

See Step 6 of *Team Problem Solving* (1995) by Sandy Pokras and Chapter 11 of *Creative Problem Solving for Managers* (2010) by Tony Proctor for additional ideas. For a theoretical foundation, see Argyris, Putnam, and Smith McLain, *Action Science* (1985).

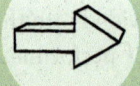

## Consider This . . .

Watching the solution take place in a well-ordered way and seeing successful evaluations have great power to restore energy and drive. Small problem or large, there is nothing like evaluating a successful result to encourage identifying the next problem, which is no doubt about to happen, with a will and confidence that solutions can be found.

# The Problem-Solver's Toolbox

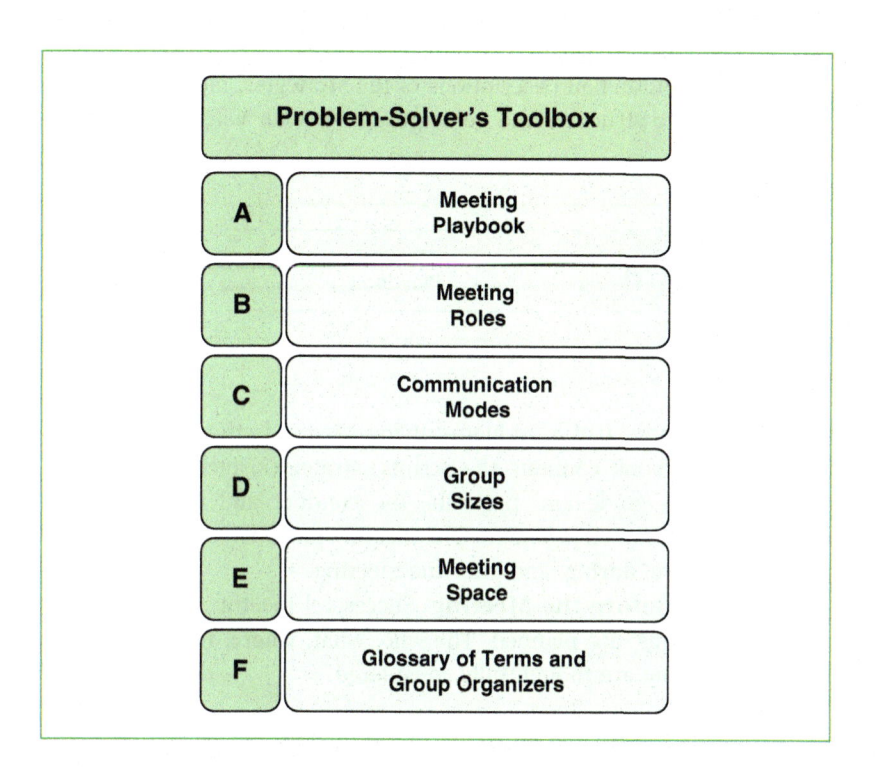

```
Problem-Solver's Toolbox
  A — Meeting Playbook
  B — Meeting Roles
  C — Communication Modes
  D — Group Sizes
  E — Meeting Space
  F — Glossary of Terms and Group Organizers
```

A toolbox is a container used to store the instruments needed to perform a task. This toolbox provides the meeting tools necessary to assist a workgroup in effectively working through the problem-solving process.

   A. *Meeting Playbook*
       The meeting outline for how problem-solving sessions will be carried out.

   B. *Meeting Roles*
       The specific jobs individual group members carry out to run an effective meeting.

   C. *Communication Modes*
       Two effective communication designs used for developing mutual understanding and promoting collaborative decision-making.

D. *Group Size*
   Group meeting designs for small, medium and large groups.

E. *Meeting Space*
   The specific configurations recommended for the physical area where the problem-solving meeting is held according to group size.

F. *Glossary Terms and Group Organizers*
   Thumbnail descriptions of the strategies, tactics, and tools used to structure and guide group behavior when meeting.

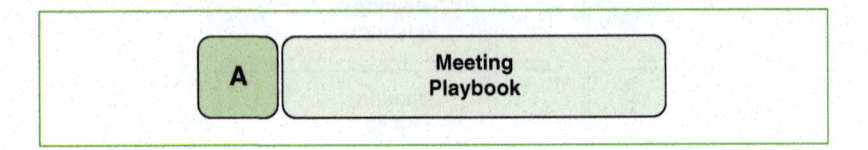

[ A — Meeting Playbook ]

An essential element of a problem-solving session is the *Meeting Playbook*. The playbook contains the scripts, strategies, tactics, tools, and techniques that guide and prescribe the conduct and content of the activity, the rules of engagement. The meeting playbook consists of three parts: the before, during, and after the meeting

**Phase 1. Before the Meeting.** Successful meetings, as with good classroom lessons, are planned. The who, what, where, when, why, and how of a meeting are thoughtfully considered.

- The purpose(s) and outcomes of the meeting are clearly defined.
- Meeting participants are identified, and their roles are assigned.
- Group processes are selected to assist participants to achieve meeting outcomes.
- Room arrangements are designed, and equipment is assembled to support group communication and participation.
- Meeting notification and meeting support materials are prepared and distributed.
- A structured agenda is built.

**Phase 2. During the Meeting.** The meeting playbook focuses on steering the proceedings.

Each meeting is a unique interpersonal interaction taking place at a unique time. The issues of the moment, both personal and professional, affect each participant attending. The social interaction occurring between and among the participants literally creates the reality of the moment. That reality can be very different from the event envisioned. Effective meetings always have "Plan Bs."

## Beginning the Meeting

- Develop icebreaker activities to center and focus participants.
- Clarify purpose and write expectation statements.
- Prepare copy of norms and ground rules.
- Build meeting agenda.

## Conducting the Meeting

- Determine process for enforcing ground rules.
- Review positive reinforcement strategies.
- Determine tactics to keep participants engaged.
- Review timing of agenda.
- Develop strategies for dealing with difficult behaviors.
- Ensure meeting space promotes effective meeting practices and provides a safe and welcoming environment for participants.

## Ending the Meeting

- Anticipate next steps.
- Prepare meeting evaluation process.
- Design process evaluation.

**Phase 3. After the Meeting.** The after-meeting playbook outlines how the meeting is evaluated. The assessment observations uncover areas for improvement and help remediate ineffective strategies and practices. These critiques often provide pathways to new and creative ways for approaching teaching and learning. The meeting evaluation provides a tool for assessing and developing group communication, collaboration, and decision-making. It also provides a snapshot of the dynamics of the group, providing a vantage point for assessing school climate and group health.

The *Meeting Playbook* for after-meeting session outlines three steps:

- Trigger process for setting the right frame of mind.
- Discrepancy analysis plan comparing plan intent with the actual experience.
- Action plan design for making corrections.

| B | Meeting Roles |

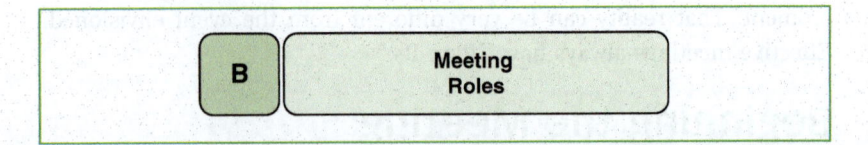

Productive meetings don't happen by chance. People structure and orchestrate these events. While traditional meeting roles focus on the presentation of the agenda, the roles of an effective meeting focus on guiding participants in productive and collaborative interactions to accomplish meeting outcomes. Meeting participants are engaged in six specific functions.

## The Meeting Manager

As the title implies, the *Meeting Manager* oversees and coordinates the creation, execution, and follow-up of the meeting. The manager is the meeting producer. This person oversees the following tasks:

- When preparing for the meeting, the *Meeting Manager* ensures there is a specific purpose and clear outcomes for the event. She or he makes sure that the right people are notified and attending.

- The *Manager* oversees the development of the agenda and the necessary materials required to support the agenda's execution.

- Depending on the type of meeting and the number of participants, the *Meeting Manager* designs and oversees the specific physical setup of the meeting venue. He or she also ensures the proper audio/video equipment is available and in operating order.

- When not assuming the role, the *Meeting Manager* appoints a facilitator to work with the group on meeting development.

- During the meeting, the *Meeting Manager's* role is essentially a supportive one. The manager works directly with the facilitator to provide additional resources as necessary.

- The manager assists the facilitator when changes in meeting structure, agenda, or purpose are required.

- The *Meeting Manager* coordinates the after-meeting evaluative activities, the next steps, an action plan, and the segues to future meetings.

In most cases the administrator in charge, the principal, dean, or department head takes on the role of *Meeting Manager*. However, the role can be delegated, depending on the specificity of meeting type and the time required to execute the role.

# The Meeting Agenda

The meeting agenda is the meeting's script, outlining the meeting's work. Most meetings are composed of three acts, the opening, the agenda items, and the closing. The agenda covers these three acts using the major headings shown in the Figure B.1.

**Figure B.1** A Sample Agenda

Meeting Title:
Meeting Type:
Meeting Data and Time:

| Agenda Item | Agenda Item Description | Person Responsible | Time Allocated | Group Process | Outcome |
|---|---|---|---|---|---|
| Preliminaries | | Facilitator | 10 minutes | • Check-In<br>• Ice Breaker<br>• Review Ground Rules<br>• Agenda Review | Group agreement |
| Item 1 | Review of follow through actions 1,2, and 3 | Participant A | 10 minutes | • Guided Discussion | Common understanding |
| Item 2 | Possible policy changes | Facilitator | 15 minutes | • Conversation | Developing a common mind-set |
| Item N | | | | | |
| Closing | | Facilitator | 15 minutes | • Agenda Review<br>• Next Steps<br>• Process Observation<br>• *Prouds and sorries*<br>• Check Out | Group closure |

A good agenda is transparent; it provides the group a detailed description of what is to transpire. As shown in Figure B.1, the agenda

- States the item or specific topic to be taken up.
- Provides a brief description of the content and the task of the item.
- Names the person guiding the process to complete the agenda item.
- Lists the time allocated for the agenda item.
- Describes the process the participants will engage in to address the agenda item in wording commonly understood by the participants.
- States the agenda item goal—its objective.

# The Facilitator

The *Facilitator* is the meeting's director. The *Facilitator*'s primary function is to guide the participants in group processes designed to support their reaching meeting outcomes. A neutral third party with no decision-making power, the *Facilitator* ensures the group's normative behavior (ground rules) and that meeting protocols are followed. *Facilitators* work to promote open communication and opportunity for equal participation by all members in a nonthreatening environment. The following are the facilitator's principal tasks (Figure B.2):

**Figure B.2**   Meeting Milestones

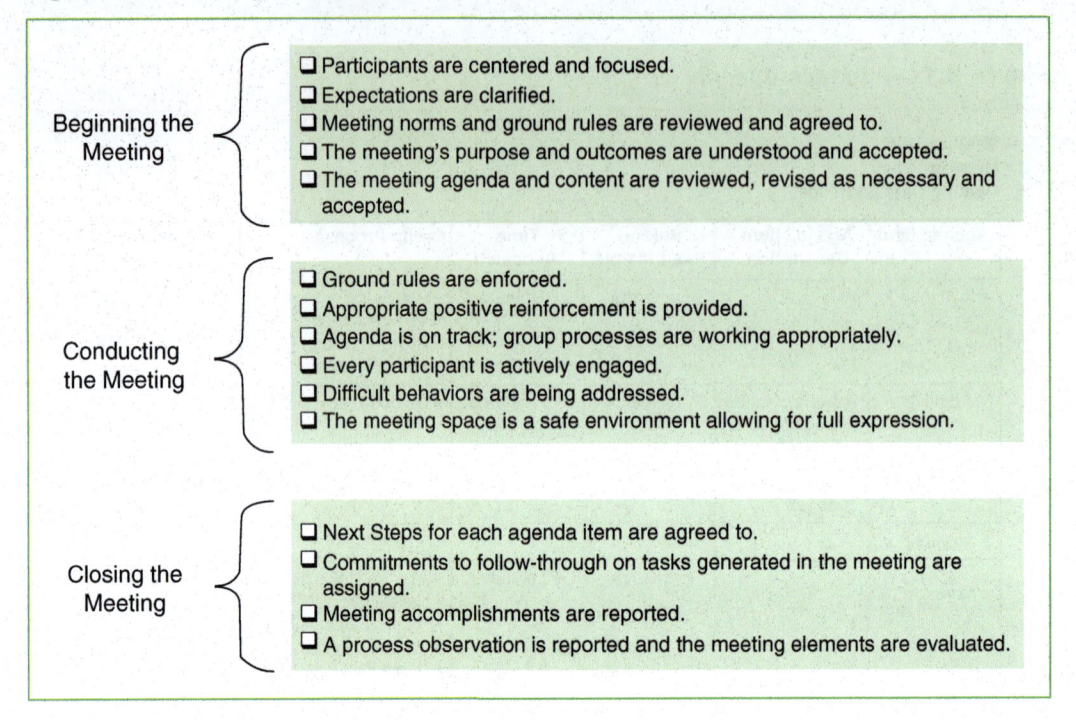

**Beginning the Meeting**
- ❏ Participants are centered and focused.
- ❏ Expectations are clarified.
- ❏ Meeting norms and ground rules are reviewed and agreed to.
- ❏ The meeting's purpose and outcomes are understood and accepted.
- ❏ The meeting agenda and content are reviewed, revised as necessary and accepted.

**Conducting the Meeting**
- ❏ Ground rules are enforced.
- ❏ Appropriate positive reinforcement is provided.
- ❏ Agenda is on track; group processes are working appropriately.
- ❏ Every participant is actively engaged.
- ❏ Difficult behaviors are being addressed.
- ❏ The meeting space is a safe environment allowing for full expression.

**Closing the Meeting**
- ❏ Next Steps for each agenda item are agreed to.
- ❏ Commitments to follow-through on tasks generated in the meeting are assigned.
- ❏ Meeting accomplishments are reported.
- ❏ A process observation is reported and the meeting elements are evaluated.

# The Recorder

The *Recorder*, as the name implies, writes the commentary of the meeting. As with the *Facilitator*, the *Recorder* is a nonparticipating neutral third party. Different than the traditional minute taker, the *Recorder* is front and center, providing a visual recount by capturing the key ideas of the group in real time. *Recorders* also assist and coach the *Facilitator* by keeping track of the information being produced. Here are the *Recorder* guidelines. The *Recorder*:

- ▶ Uses an easel and flipchart or whiteboard and scribes, as accurately as possible, a visual outline of what is being said in the meeting, jotting down the key words and phrases being used in the conversation.

- ▶ When necessary, can paraphrase or reframe the comments for clarity.

- ▶ Prints in big letters so that all participants can clearly see what's being written.

- ▶ Since the writing is on the fly, abbreviates wherever possible—spelling and grammar are discounted.

- When unsure, asks the group to either slow down or repeat what's being said to ensure an accurate accounting of the proceedings.
- Records all key agreements and ideas and highlights them.
- Since the meeting proceeding will be contained on multiple sheets, numbers each page and posts completed pages in prominence so a visual meeting memory is provided for all attendees.

## The Flipchart

The *Flipchart* is a primary meeting tool and is the focal point for the meeting proceedings. The information contained on the *Flipchart* pages serves as the *Group Memory*. It is used as a reference to chronicle the group's work and is the record that documents the meeting history. The *Flipchart* serves four functions; it is a learning device, a focusing device, a meeting tool, and the group's memory.

- As a learning device, the *Flipchart* provides a powerful aid for visual learners, enabling them to track the conversation.
- The *Flipchart* should provide a clear, readable, and trackable commentary of the meeting proceedings and be clearly visible to all participants.
- The *Flipchart* is also a focusing device. The meeting's play-by-play action is replicated on its sheets so that all can keep track of what occurring.
- It is a meeting tool providing the primary meeting technology; it displays the record of the conversation and charts the work product of the meeting.
- The *Flipchart* can be used to assist the group to advance organize. It can be used to help draft appropriate wording, compare various options, and connect different ideas.
- It is the *Group Memory*. The recording of the meeting is the contemporaneous record of the group's problem solving, decision-making, and conflict management as it occurs.
- The *Flipchart* provides a historical record. The *Group Memory* is a primary account of the meeting used for the evaluation and historical record.

## The Process Observer

The participants' self-assessment is an essential part of the meeting. When meeting participants become metacognitive about meeting performance and adjust their behavior accordingly, the group becomes more cohesive and the meeting processes and structures become more efficient and effective.

Given the importance of this evaluative process, the role of *Process Observer* was created. The *Process Observer* is to observe and document the meeting leaders and participant behaviors, group health, and group productivity. Based on the data accumulated, the *Observer* provides feedback to the group at meeting's end, a meeting report card. As with the other meeting roles, *Process Observers* are neutral third parties and do not participate in meeting activities.

The *Process Observer* watches the who, the how, and the what of the meeting. This person observes the way each participant communicates and participates in the group.

Meeting participation is also observed at the group level to determine how the group is communicating, participating, and interacting. Specifically, the *Process Observer* is looking for the following:

- Open, honest, nonjudgmental, respectful, and unfettered conversation.

- Communication that divides or prevents the group from moving the agenda forward, such as debate or argument, is noted.

- Group cohesion. Is there group cooperation, or is the group splintered and divided?

- Group support. Is the group promoting equal treatment to all? Is there a healthy and safe environment for each participant?

- The quality and effectiveness of the facilitator and the recorder. Particular attention is paid to adherence to the normative behavior and ground rules agreed to by the group.

- How effective are group processing tools, the decision-making, and the consensus-building actions of the group?

- Are the human needs of the group met?

- How productive was the group? Task and outcome completion is tallied and described. A summarization of agenda completion is reported.

- The effectiveness of the physical arrangement of the room and technologies used are noted, pointing out their efficiencies and deficiencies.

The function of the *Process Observer* is not an evaluative one. Efficiencies and deficiencies are only noted based on pre-agreed criteria. On the completion of the *Process Observer's* remarks, meeting participants can ask for clarification and definition. Process observations can be made during the meeting as well. This type of intervention is agreed to by all participants in advance and is established in the ground rules.

The Problem-Solver's Toolbox    **141**

| C | Communication Modes |

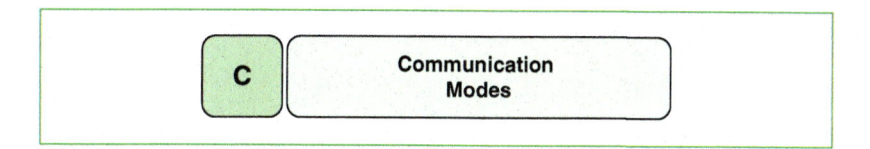

Work of the group is transacted through communications. We, in the United States, make it a standard practice to engage in various forms of bad communication. Due to our competitive nature, we engage in stating positions and promoting our positions rather than sharing information to gain a common understanding. When a group is communicating poorly, regardless of the intention of its members, outcomes produced by the group are impaired, resulting in ineffective decision-making and problem solving. However, groups can communicate very effectively when engaging in intercommunication modes that encourage common sense making and collaboration. Here is one way to look at the various modes of communication and what they do. Know the one you're having.

**Figure C.1**  Modes of Group Communication

| Communication Mode | Argument | Debate | Discourse | Conversation | Skilled Discussion | Dialogue |
|---|---|---|---|---|---|---|
| Purpose | Overpower | Win | Convince | Exchange | Seek Common Ground | Explore |
| Disposition | Emotional | Rational/Strategic | Positional | Contribute | Collaborate | Inquisitive |
| Interaction | Forcing | Reasoning | Telling | Reacting | Contributing | Co-creating |

"I" Communication — Communication is closed, assertive, positional, and competitive.

"We" Communication — Communication is open, consensual, inclusive, and collaborative.

As can be seen in Figure C.1, group communications are divided into two types, "I" and "We" communications.

*"I" Communications* are egocentric. They express a self-view, the world from my perspective. Since they're ego-centered, they are closed communications, propositional in nature. These are one-way communications that mean to sustain and defend the position of the sender. They are assertive and competitive, resulting in either/or, win/

lose decision-making. The four major modes of "I" communications are as follows:

- *Argument.* An exchange of untethered emotional monologues meant to overpower another with the aim of neutralizing the other party. Arguments are usually fight/flight responses.
- *Debate.* A two-way exchange addressing a question or particular topic in which logical arguments are put forward to win the conversation. The arguments are positional and biased.
- *Discourse.* A one-way exchange that authoritatively expresses a position on a particular topic or question meaning to inform or convince the other party.
- *Conversation.* A familiar two-way exchange of ideas and thoughts, usually informal in nature. Parties contribute individual viewpoints adding to and reacting to the previous comments.

"We" *communications* are concentric. They seek to understand and to express a worldview and understanding based on multiple perspectives and vantage points, the world from our view. They are open communications seeking inclusivity and common understanding. Collaborative in nature, they lead to common agreements and consensus in decision-making.

- *Skilled discussion.* A collaborative two-way exchange where parties seek to understand and include all viewpoints to reach closure for the purpose of making a decision or reaching an agreement.
- *Dialog.* A communal two-way exchange meant to explore ideas and opinions for the purpose of co-creating a new understanding.

## The Collaborative Participant

Group members successful at conducting collaborative communication must be intentional, reflective, and skilled. Rick Ross in the text *The Fifth Discipline Field Book* suggested the five behaviors are required when engaging in collaborative communications.

1. Pay attention to your intentions.

    A member joins the group with the intention to collaborate and to work toward consensual solutions. This is not automatic; most group members must prompt themselves into this behavior.

They need to trigger their "we" side, committing to acting and thinking in a collaborative fashion.

2. Balance advocacy with inquiry.

   Group members must be comfortable being able to say it as they see it. Members have a duty to take positions on the issues before the group. In the context of rational problem solving, such opinions are reasoned. The positions taken must be backed by facts logically arranged as evidence, which logically lead to the position taken. Advocacy of a position is an essential part of a collaborative effort but represents only half of the equation. Members must advocate their position but must also actively seek to understand the positions of others. The other half of the collaborative effort is inquiry. In addition to honestly advocating one's position, every group member must be of an open mind seeking to inquire in order to understand what others are seeing in order to capture the ideas of the many.

3. Build shared meaning.

   Creating a group understanding of an issue or situation begins with a common understanding about what is being seen or felt. This is not an automatic—in fact, the opposite is true. Differing viewpoints and vantage points create differing views, differing definitions, and descriptions. Groups see things differently until they make the effort to see the in the same way—that is, build shared meaning. Building shared meaning is a stereoscopic process that creates a multi-dimensional view of what's been seen. Shared meaning is built by an additive process, where each viewpoint is considered expanding the definition either by qualifying or corroborating it until all are satisfied with the outcome.

4. Each member participates, focusing on the present and his or her behavior in that present. Acting mindful means participants:

   - Have reviewed all preparatory materials relating to the agenda and have a clear understanding of them.

   - Understand their role in contributing to the purpose and the output of the meeting.

   - Are prepared to seek clarification where ambiguity occurs and to suggest additions or amendments to the agenda as they see appropriate.

   - Avoid distraction—whether physical, emotional, or other.

   - Work to maintain a positive attitude and actively work to contribute ideas.

   - Practice active listening—suspending judgment and seeking clarification or definition about issues or ideas that are unclear.

- Avoid being defensive; seek to understand the reasoning behind what is being suggested.
- Make commitments to ideas and actions when required.
- When speaking, work at being brief and concise, always being conscious of the unwritten rule of "sharing airtime."
- Work hard at avoiding interrupting or cutting off another person's comments; side conversations and commentary should be avoided completely.

5. Explore impasses. The normal responses to an impasse are fight, flight, or castle. When an impasse arises, rather than arguing positions, overpowering or acceding to power, or retreating and standing firm on an issue, explore avenues of consensus and conciliation. The group moves from the "either/or" arguments to "both/and thinking," the integration of various vantage points and viewpoints, even when disparate or opposing. The intent of the exploration effort is to get the entire elephant in the room. Once done, determine the sticking points and the inflexibility of positions and the reasons for the inflexibility. Seek fixes and detours. Work hard at forging compromises when consensual agreements are not forthcoming. Solve what can be solved, and leave the rest in the parking lot to be considered at predetermined latter date or when conditions change. Keep the discussion focused on the issue and not the person.

## Conducting a Skillful Discussion

The perquisites and general principles for a skillful discussion are described in Chapter 2 and in the other sections of the Toolbox. The five behaviors suggested by Rick Ross just discussed are musts.

### Purpose

A skillful discussion is a collaborative conversation with a purpose. It is conducted to build shared meaning, gain common agreement, analyze and evaluate, or make a decision.

### Description

The participants sit at round tables with no more than eight to a table. Table participants can be randomly placed, placed by "job alike," or placed across job function, depending on the nature of the question and outcome sought. The facilitator stands center stage, and the recorder positions flipcharts so all have an unimpeded view. Where the group is eight or fewer, the facilitator sits at the table. Participants exercise the five behaviors of the collaborative participant. The facilitator leads the discussion using guiding questions and suggestions for next steps. The recorder transcribes the proceedings so all can follow and refers to what has been said. If rules or norms are violated, the process observer stops the discussion and points out the violation. The facilitator works the group through a remediation and the process proceeds. The discussion continues until the outcome is reached. A time period is established for completion of the activity. If the outcome is not reached by the expiration of time, the group can agree to extend time.

## Procedure

The following describes how a skillful discussion is conducted.

1. Set the stage

    The facilitator presents the purpose and intended outcome of the session and gains agreement from the group to proceed. The rules, norms, and procedures of a skillful discussion are reviewed, and group members agree to engage in the process. Time is set for the duration of the proceedings.

2. Establish the safe zone

    Group members are asked to reflect on the purpose of the session and how they are to collaboratively participate. Meditation or guided imagery techniques can be employed here.

3. Conduct the session

    The facilitator presents a focus question beginning the discussion on the session's purpose. The discussion is assisted using Group Organizers or guided facilitation until the outcome is reached, or time is exhausted. The recorder actively transcribes the conversation, reporting out to the group when recall or clarification is required.

4. Conclude the session

    The process observer presents observations on the proceedings. The group reflects on the remarks. The facilitator leads the group in a "prouds and sorrys" and asks for recommendations for session improvement. The facilitator thanks and compliments the group, concluding the session.

# Conducting a Dialog

As with the skillful discussion, the general meeting principles described in Chapter 2, the Five Behaviors and other elements of the Toolbox are prerequisites here as well.

## Purpose

Creating a dialog is a collaborative conversation's purpose. It is to explore, expand, and embellish the group's understanding of the topic using the processes of reflective speaking, questioning, and listening.

## Description

Participants sit in a circle. The dialog leader frames the question. Participants engage in the dialog as they are moved. There is no sequential order to the participation. Recorder can be used as needed. Questions and nonjudgmental statements are used to expand the group's understanding of the topic dialog, which continues until the time is lapsed or participants have completed their contributions. Differing from all other modes of communication, dialogs are nonjudgmental and non-positional. Members of the dialog "speak their truths." At no point in the dialog do members refute or contradict previous comments. Dialog then extends or expands the conversation.

## Procedure

1. Set the stage. The group leader poses the focus question. The dialogical process is explained and agreed to by participants. The group then reflects on the nuances and possibilities presented by the question. The reflection period concludes with group members considering the manner in which they will join the dialog: what questions they will pull, how they will contribute statements to the dialog, and how they will actively listen.

2. Conduct the dialog. The dialog leader restates the focus question and invites the members into the dialog. The dialog begins and continues until the allotted time is expended or participant interaction is completed. The recorder is employed, as necessary, to transcribe the contributions of the participants.

3. Concluding the dialog. At the completion of the dialog, the leader asks the group to reflect on the proceedings, thank all participants for their contributions, and ask the group to celebrate their work.

| D | Group Sizes |
|---|---|

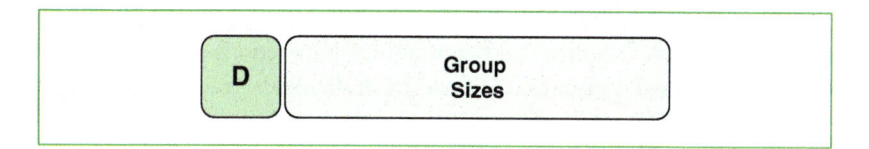

Two foundational principles provide the rationale for group-meeting design. They are the ideas of voice and choice and total group involvement. Space configurations, the use of facilitation, ground rules and norms, and employing Group Organizers are all focused to meet these principles. The procedure by which meetings are conducted also applies to this rationale. So small-, medium-, and large-sized groups use different procedures.

## Small-Group Meeting Procedures

The small-group (2–6 members) procedures abbreviate the process and procedures used by a medium-sized group. Since most small groups are informal and familial in nature, skillful discussions are the mainstay of their processes. The use of dyads and triads as well as most Group Organizers are not necessary. Small groups will benefit from the use of organizers—like the 3Cs or the P. I. D. process for their analytical capabilities. For the most part, however, the group discusses as a whole.

## Medium-Sized Group Meeting Procedures

The procedures for medium-sized groups (7–12 members) have been addressed by the Task Cue Cards in each of the chapters.

## Large-Sized Group Meeting Procedures

There is a place for principal's meetings, faculty meetings, and district-wide meetings. The same goes for higher education's dean's meetings, department or schoolwide meetings, and faculty synods. In the main, they all suffer from the extreme overuse of show and tell, a malady that is fatal. However, there are times when problem solving and decision-making require the whole group be in the room, when the synergy and wisdom of the whole group is the most efficient and effective way to proceed. It is the best way to meet when the stakeholders are the entire group and each member's voice needs to be heard to gain a solution and generate buy-in for the course of action chosen. It is "we" involvement at its best, when it is designed well. Such meetings are the best choices when dealing with strategic planning, futuring, scenario building, and community problem-solving sessions.

The more complicated situations dealing with strategic planning, futuring, scenario building, and community interactions should be conducted by trained facilitators. These are individuals trained to employ sophisticated, large-scale interactive processes with an entire organization. For most of these opportunities, however, the "accordion process design" can be integrated into the meeting strategies suggested for the medium-sized groups to create a robust strategy for a large-group interaction. Here are the basics.

The Divergence/Convergence process facilitates group member "Voice and Choice."

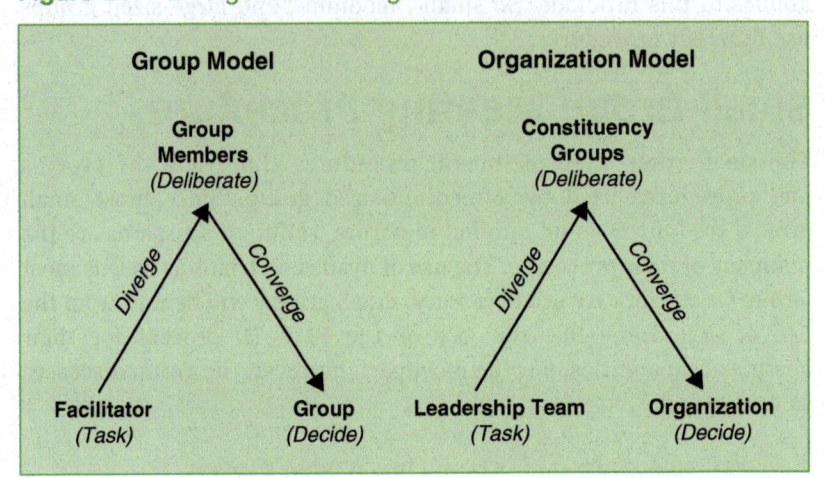

**Figure D.1** Divergence/Convergence Process

**Group Model**
- Group Members (Deliberate)
- Diverge / Converge
- Facilitator (Task)
- Group (Decide)

**Organization Model**
- Constituency Groups (Deliberate)
- Diverge / Converge
- Leadership Team (Task)
- Organization (Decide)

"Voice and choice" is the bedrock principle driving participatory problem solving and decision-making. *Voice* allows differing vantage points and points of view to be in the room. *Choice* allows the many to participate in decisions being made. Giving voice is a divergent process while allowing choice is a convergent process. As can be seen in the chapter's Task Cue Cards, moving from task to solution incorporates a series of divergent/convergent processes until a task is completed. Groups and whole organizations engaging participatory decision-making and problem-solving use divergence/convergence process as graphically depicted in Figure D.1.

> Group model. The *Facilitator* sets task, purpose, and outcome. A facilitator uses one or more *Group Organizers* to get *group members'* various viewpoints and positions into the discussion. Using the results of that divergent process, the *Facilitator* then uses *Group Organizers* to assist *group members* to reach a common understanding, develop common meaning, or come to a common agreement. The *group* completes the task using convergent procedures.

▶ Organization model. As with whole-organizations, the processes are the same. The difference is groups rather than individuals generate the work. As previously shown in Figure D.1, the *Leadership Team* facilitates the task, purpose, and outcome. Group Organizers are designed to elicit the various viewpoints and positions of the constituent groups. Individual groups process their work and then report out. The leadership team then leads the constituent groups, as a whole, using Group Organizers to converge ideas. The whole organization is now participating in developing the outcome. Here is how the whole organization process looks.

**Figure D.2** Large Group Process

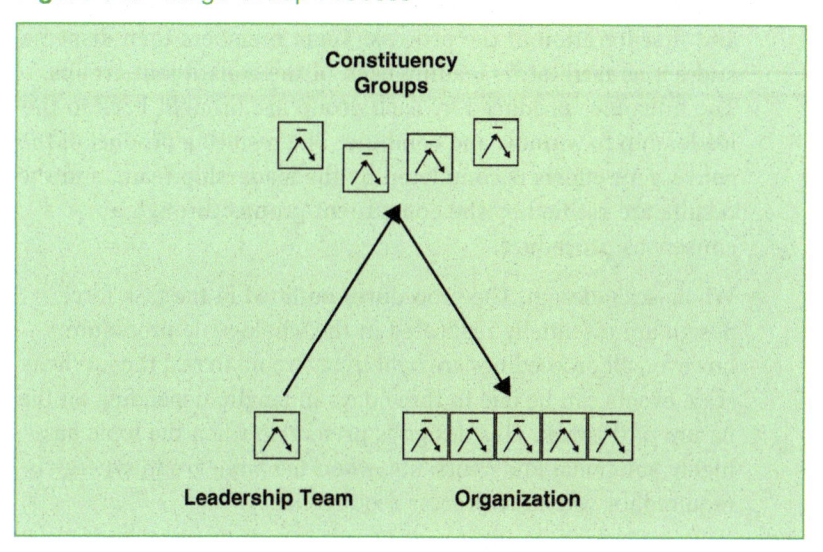

## The Accordion Process

**Figure D.3** The Accordion Process

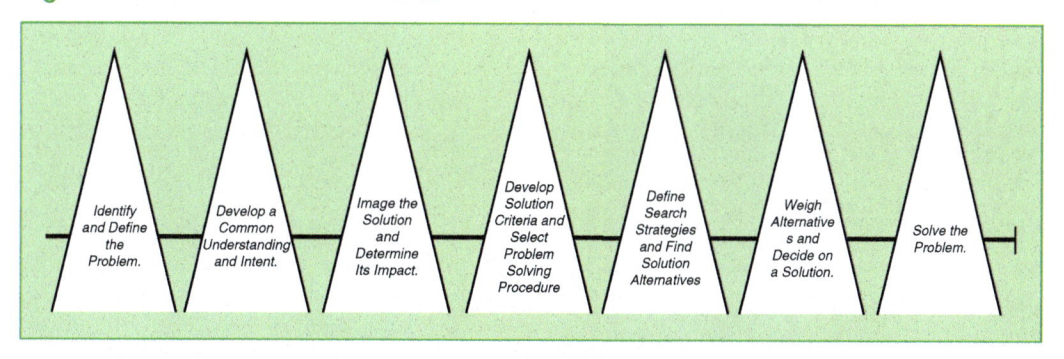

Large groups can function as a medium-sized group through the use of the "accordion process," so named because of the in-and-out nature caused by the successive iterations, the team's divergent and convergent episodes. Figure D.3 depicts the accordion process for the problem-solving process. Each step of the process is carried out according to the design as shown in Figure D.2. Leadership teams organize and facilitate the work of the constituency groups and the group at large. As each step is completed, the next iteration of the accordion begins.

The two ways the accordion process can be designed. They are the following:

- The task-force design. This design uses a field-based strategy. The leadership team meets and works through the game plan and first iteration of the process. Team members then disperse and act as facilitators leading each of the constituent groups. The outcomes produced by each group are brought back to the leadership to winnow and combine. The resulting product of the convergent efforts is completed by the leadership team, and the results are ratified by the constituent groups through a consensus procedure.

- Whole-scale design. The procedures outlined in the task-force design are essentially replicated in the whole-scale procedure; however, all proceedings are held in one room in real time. Whole-scale events can be one to three days in length, depending on the nature of the task. This design is preferable when the topic has highly emotional undercurrents, when the large group synergy is required, or when the process requires it.

| E | Meeting Space |

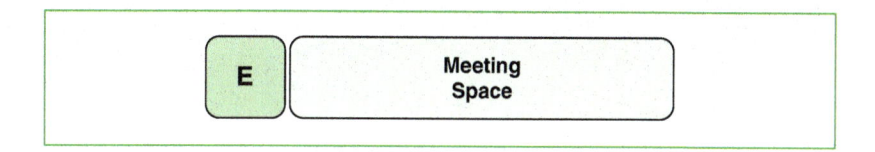

Just a few words about space. Have the space work for collaborative interactions, not against it.

- Tables are round, period. Everyone can see and interact with each other. No more than ten to a table.
- Comfortable chairs.
- Technology works. Always check beforehand. No dead batteries or internet drops.
- Have wall space to hang completed flipchart sheets. You want the visual history of the meeting to be seen and referred back to by participants.
- Good lighting and HVAC.
- Space protected from outside interference.
- Room has Wi-Fi and charging capability.
- Good sound system is a must in large-group settings.

## Basic Setting

As shown in Figure E.1, the basic meeting configuration is a round table and comfortable chairs. Necessary supplies should be placed on table. Technology should be readily available. Flipcharts can be stand-alones or tabletop, depending on table and group size. Human needs—such as coffee, tea, and healthy snacks—should be close by. This is the basic design for small- and medium-sized groups.

**Figure E.1** Basic Unit

# Large Group Settings

**Figure E.2** Large-Group Configuration

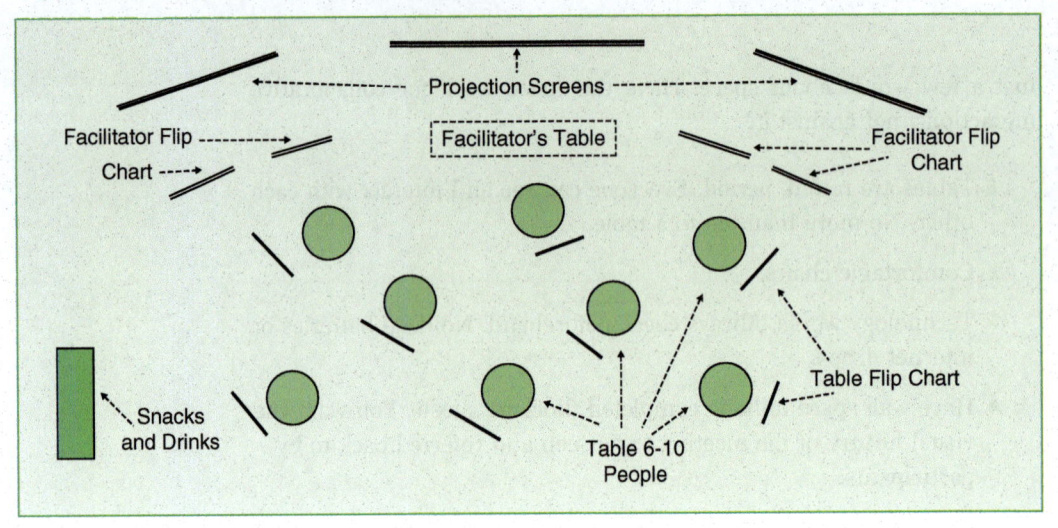

*[Diagram showing large-group room configuration with: Projection Screens at top center, Facilitator's Table below screens, Facilitator Flip Charts on left and right sides, round tables (6-10 People) arranged in the participant space, Table Flip Charts near tables, and Snacks and Drinks area on the left side]*

The interactive large-group setting should be designed to be as intimate as possible. Table spacing should neither be too tight or too far apart (4- to 6-foot separation, if possible). Room size should accommodate the group size. Don't cramp or have large excess space. As shown in Figure E.2, the room is divided into three sections: facilitator space, participants space, and needs spaces.

▶ *The facilitator spaces* are at the head of the room.
- Projection screens must be large enough to be easily viewed by participants at the rear of the room and placed strategically on the back wall.
- Ensure lighting enhances screen clarity and does not create a dulling effect.
- Forward of the screen are the facilitator's flipcharts, supplied with multi-colored pens. The number varies with the number of recorders and the complexity of the session. Whiteboards can be used as well.
- Upstage center is the facilitator's table. The table can house technology and facilitator supplies.
- Notice, there is no podium. Meeting facilitation is best done by being in-group and not behind a podium.

- *The participant's spaces* are located in the center of the room.
  - Round tables large enough to accommodate 10 people comfortably are distributed in the center area and are positioned in such a way that each table has as clear a view to the head of the room as possible.
  - Outfit each table with comfortably wide chairs.
  - Display table flipcharts for all to see.
- *Human needs area* is located at the rear of the room.
  - Close proximity to the participants area but far enough away to pose no interference with proceedings.
  - Ensure refreshments are ample and always available.
  - Restrooms should be close to venue with easy access. Make sure signage is visible.

> **F** | **Glossary of Terms and Group Organizers**

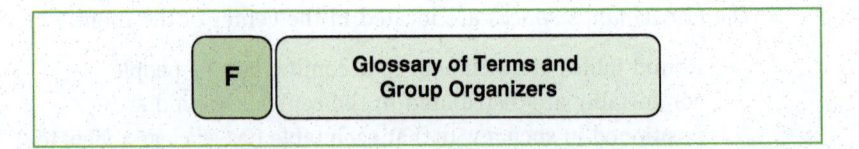

Please note: Glossary F contains entries defining key terms and thumbnail descriptions of the Group Organizers used in this text. Reference titles for the Group Organizers will be in *italics* to differentiate them from the key terms.

## Action Learning

Action learning is a metacognitive process where participant groups study their own actions and experiences in order to improve performance. Action learning is a three-step process: a reflection on what is, an assessment of what should be, and the building or finding of a solution that satisfies the "should be" conditions. What did we do? How did it work? What do we do next? The outcome of this reflection should guide the group's future actions and improve the group's performance.

## Action Plans

An *Action Plan* is a Group Organizer that structures the steps necessary to facilitate a task or tasks. The result of the action-planning process is a record of information describing how the plan will be implemented. The *Action Plan* describes the action to be completed, the key people involved, the lead person, resources required to complete the action, evaluation requirements, timeframe, and date to be completed.

## Administrivia

These are administrative and management tasks regarded as trivial, boring, and time-consuming. The inference is that these tasks are not worth the effort and should be delegated out.

## Blue Skying

Using your imagination to think of things that have not yet been created.

## Brainstorming

Originally conceived by Alex Osborn, *Brainstorming* is an informal discussion in which the group engages in lateral thinking in a free-form and free-flow process. Its purpose is to create as many ideas as possible. In brainstorming, there are no bad ideas. The discussion is nonjudgmental and is supportive of member's input. Divergent ideas are encouraged regardless of how off-center they might be. The more creative the idea, the better. Thinking outside of the box is encouraged. The goal of *Brainstorming* is to shake the group out of its present thinking and generate as many ideas as possible.

## Clarification Process

Clarifying is a communication practice used to explore the positions taken by group members. Paraphrasing statements are made to check for understanding, and exploratory questions are posed to clarify and further expand the ideas presented. Prompts such as I hear you saying …; I am hearing you say …; am I understanding you to mean? can be used to engage the conversation.

## Consensus Process

Consensus is a process of getting substantial agreement from the group so an action or a position can be taken. Three elements make up a consensual agreement. They are the following: all members understand the problem; all members agree that they've been heard; and all members agree to support the solution whether they are in agreement with it or not.

- The consensus process begins by presenting the action or position to be considered.

- A round-robin procedure is conducted querying each member's understanding of the solution. Once completed, members can clarify issues or misunderstandings. Based on the discussion, the action is revised and reduced to writing.

- The final statement is read aloud and the group is polled for agreement. Members can respond by (1) agreeing to support the solution, (2) agreeing to allow the solution to go forward without personal resistance, or (3) disagreeing to support the solution at this time.

- If the polling results in members voting to agree or not resist moving the solution forward, then a consensus has been reached.

- When one or more members disagree to support the solution, further discussion takes place. Dissenting members are asked, "What changes need to occur for the solution go to forward? The group works with the individual until a common agreement can be made. The solution is amended accordingly.

## Contingency Planning

A contingency plan is an alternative course of action used when the plan in motion fails or a preplanned option to be employed is based on the unknown turn of future events. The alternate plan, Plan B, is developed when creating the preferable course of action. The preplanned contingency plans can be based on "what/if" scenarios predicting the best, worst, and most likely scenarios to occur. They can also be based on "if this/then this" scenarios, where alternative futures are known. Contingency plans are created in four steps. Determine the desired outcome. Determine what can go wrong when trying to achieve it. Determine the solution required to counteract the difficulties. Finally, determine what actions are needed to achieve the solution. The actions developed in the last step become the elements of the contingency plan.

### Counting 3-2-1

This simple strategy for weighing alternatives assigns value based on the priority designation of the criterion. A *Must* having the greatest priority is assigned a *3*; a *Preference* is assigned a value of *2*, and a *Nice To* a value of *1*. Solution options that meet criterion standards are given the numerical rating corresponding to their priority. Once all criteria have been assessed and rated, the scores are tallied and totaled. The solution option scoring the highest number of points is selected as the optimum choice.

## Crisis Management Plan

A crisis management plan is a blueprint for how the organization will respond to and resolve a crisis. It describes the actions needed to be taken and the individuals or groups who will be involved. A crisis management plan can be divided into three stages, contain, control, and construct—the 3Cs. Solution responses are developed for each stage. *Contain:* assessments are conducted to assess the type and urgency of the problem; stop-gap solutions are developed to temporarily contain and stabilize the situation. *Control:* trial solutions are developed using trial and error or bootstrapping techniques to define the problem situation to explore best alternative solutions. Once identified, solutions evolve until the situation is controlled. *Construct:* using the findings of the second phase, solution criteria are generated, alternative solutions are collected, and a solution, or solutions, are chosen to resolve the situation. The application of the 3Cs process can differ depending on what is known about the *difficulty of the crisis problem* (see Chapter 2, Task 3). Plans can be anticipatory, proactive, or reactive depending upon the knowledge of the crisis problem and prior preparation by the organization.

### Dialog

The thoughtful exchange of ideas between two people. As a group organizer, the *Dialog* is a reflective conversation designed to share meaning and explore new ideas. The basic dialogical process can be described as follows: Participants sit in the circle. The dialog leader frames the question. Participants enter into a *Dialog* as they are moved. There is no sequence of order to the participation. A recorder can be used as needed. Participants use questions and nonjudgmental statements to expand the group's understanding of the topic. *Dialog* continues until time has lapsed or participants complete their input. At the completion of the *Dialog,* the leader asks the group to reflect on the proceedings. The leader thanks all participants for their contributions and asks the group to celebrate their work.

## Descriptive Rubric

A descriptive rubric is a qualitative evaluation instrument. It is a rating scale that describes the levels of performance or completion of a task or process based on preset criteria. Levels of performance can be divided into categories such as, meets standards, partially meets standards, exceeds standards, and so forth. A concise statement describing each of the gradations of performance is written for each of the criteria forming a grid. The gradations of criteria contained in the rubric are compared to the actual task or process being performed and evaluated accordingly.

## Differentiating

Identifying the differences between two or more things.

### Discrepancy Analysis Process

A *Discrepancy Analysis* or *Gap Analysis* is an analytical procedure that examines the difference between actual state and desired state (what is vs. what should be). The difference between the two is the discrepancy. Identifying the elements that make up the discrepancy allow decision-makers the ability to determine an appropriate solution. The procedure for conducting a *Discrepancy Analysis* works as follows:

- Ask the participants to define the actual state. Use the 5Ws.
- Once the actual state is defined and commonly understood, participants define the ideal state. This can be accomplished using creative brainstorming processes.
- Next, the group examines, describes, and defines the differences (gaps) between the actual and desired state.
- Last, the group analyzes the gap and descriptions to build elements of a solution.

### Dyads and Triads

*Dyads and Triads* are active listening processes designed to improve communication and elicit shared understanding through clarification. These processes are often used in groups to build definition or position using an accordion process.

The procedure for conducting a *Dyad* is as follows:

- Two people enter a discussion based on a predefined focus question.
- The first person, the speaker, responds to the focus question.
- The second person, the listener, listens to what being said with the intent of repeating and confirming that information. Additionally, the listener queries the speaker on points in need of clarification to extend and further define what has been said.
- Once this process is completed, a second-round conversation commences with participants reversing rules.
- Once both rounds have been completed, the dyad reports out what they have learned to the group.

*Triads* work as follows:

- Similar to a *Dyad*, the first person, the speaker, responds to the focus question.
- The second person, the listener, interacts with the speaker by questioning to clarify, extend, and expand the speaker's position.
- The third person, the observer, listens to the discussion, and at the end of the round, confirms the content and comments on the quality of the conversation.
- As with the *Dyad*, *Triad* participants exchange roles through rounds until all have spoken. The result of the conversation is reported out to the whole group.

## Formative Evaluation

Formative evaluation measures progress and the quality of program initiatives as they are being implemented. Evaluators gather information regarding the quality of efforts, progress toward intended outcome, and fidelity of the implementation to the plan (actual vs. intended). Differences and deficiencies are noted and reported back to staff for the purposes of remediating deficiencies and improving program implementation.

## 4Ds

The 4Ds is a four-step process used for creative problem solving.

*Discover*. Clarify and define the problem. Learn as much as possible about the problem by searching out similar situations from outside sources. Gather salient facts. Construct the problem from what has been learned. Picture the desired end state. Look at the desired conditions from various angles. Look at both the should bes and could bes. Identify and define the processes and outcomes of the desired future. In this phase, explore all opportunities. Think out of the box.

*Dream.* Using the results of the *Discovery,* employ imaging techniques to imagine what the solution would look like. Envision the 5Ws of this new world. Create the picture. Dreaming has four phases: *preparation,* gathering information on the desired end state; *incubation,* using free flow thinking to imagine what the potential end state might look like and produce; *illumination,* the crystallizing moment where ideas form a picture, creating a path to the solution; *verification,* is the dream doable?

*Design.* Realize the picture. Integrating the products of Steps 1 and 2, devise a solution based upon the results produced in the *Dream* phase. Ensure the solution produced creates outcomes that meet or exceed those defined in the *Discovery* phase. From the template that emerges, design the structures, procedures, and elements necessary to make the dream a reality.

*Do.* Implement the action planning necessary to make the design operational. In this phase, combine best past practices with imagined creative practices to implement the initiative.

## Gallery Walk

The *Gallery Walk* is a Group Organizer used to multitask. Subgroups are used to define specific segments of a problem or can be used to provide diverse viewpoints about an issue. Here's how it works:

- Divide the large group into smaller groups based upon organization purpose like job likes, sociological purpose—like gender-based—or by random selection.

- Second, subgroups groups are sent to stations, either at corners of a large room or to assigned breakout rooms. There they complete an assignment given to the group. A designated amount of time is given to complete the task.

- Third, when time is up, breakout groups reconvene in the large setting and are formed into "tour groups."

- Four, the tour groups visit each station where a representative explains the flipcharts to the tour group and answers any questions posed.

- Once all groups have completed the walk, they return to the main room for discussion and the next task.

## Gap Analysis (See Discrepancy Analysis Process)
## Group Organizers

Group Organizers are processes and techniques that order the way groups think and decide together. They are mental structuring devices that allow a group to work collaboratively to a single objective.

### Imaging

Imaging is the process of creating a visual representation of something by forming a mental image or picture of it. The imaging process depicts some future state by envisioning mental models of that state from various vantage points and possibilities. The structure, people, and abstract aspects of the model are portrayed through the use of metaphor, archetype, or future scenario techniques.

### Mind Mapping

A *Mind Map* is a freeform depiction that graphically represents the various parts of a topic. Originated by Tony Buzan, the *Mind Map* is a technique used to capture the free flow and random thoughts members of the group have about a topic. These thoughts are recorded by a common idea, categorized by thread, and organized to eventually outline a construct.

Here's how the *Mind Mapping* process works:

- The group develops and agrees to a common definition of the topic of the map. This key idea is the central topic, which is placed in the center of the map.

- As new ideas and concepts are voiced, they are recorded as threads or subtopics by classification.

- Once depicted, relationships are drawn between the subtopics.

Symbols, graphics, colors and various styles of writing are used to embellish the map and create deeper meaning. While the map may be posted on a single flipchart, it is highly recommended the map be big enough to comfortably depict all ideas.

### Mindscaping

The purpose of this process is to create a visual map of an environment from a holistic perspective. *Mindscaping* draws on the creative intuition of the participants. The group's task is to visualize the landscape of the idea in question. As with a landscape, all the salient features of the of the idea are described in detail using graphics, pictures, and diagrams. The goal here is to describe the idea visually as well as viscerally. A *Mindscape* should be evocative, presenting both a visual and emotional depiction of the topic. Chart paper, colored pens and pencils, sticky notes, pictures from magazines, or graphics are made available for participants to use. The time allocation for this activity depends on the topic and the group's capability. Here is a *Mindscape* procedure:

- Assemble materials on a table or tables to be readily available for use by participants. Post a $3 \times 8$ piece of paper on the wall in plain view and with easy access to all members of the group. Place the materials table in front of the chart, and position participant chairs surrounding the three outside of the table.

- Distribute creative materials to each member of the group. Review the principles of *Mindscape*.

- Present the focus question. Write the question in the chart's center and circle it. Check for group understanding. Allow an appropriate reflective time for group members to imagine and consider ways to respond.

- After an appropriate time, group members begin to create responses using the materials provided. This is done in extemporaneous and freeform fashion. Global thinking is encouraged. As threads of ideas are put forward, relationships can be built by hearing other people's ideas and expanding on them. It's okay to be messy. As members are participating in building the landscape, facilitators can ask encouraging questions to increase depth and complexity in the project.

- The process continues until time has elapsed or until project participants are satisfied with what they have created.

## Nominal Group Technique

The *Nominal Group Technique* is a formalized or structured alternative to *Brainstorming*. This device is used to balance group participation and ensure that all voices have been heard. It is an ideal Group Organizer to use when groups are diverse or have different personal agendas that may be causing a group conflict or controversy. Here's how it works:

- To begin, the leader presents the issue or decision under discussion and then gives group members a few minutes to think about the question posed.

- Next, group members generate responses transcribing them to a piece of paper, 3 × 5 cards or sticky notes. Once members have completed writing down their ideas, those responses are gathered from each individual in a round-robin style and recorded on the flipchart.

- When all ideas have been posted, the group addresses each item seeking clarification and shared meaning.

- A *Winnowing* process is conducted, which combines or eliminates ideas to the final list.

- The final list is then voted on by the members using the following procedure: Using a 3 × 5 card or sticky note, each member writes down five ideas from the list he or she considers to be the best. The 3 × 5 cards are then passed to the group leader, and the votes on the best ideas or solutions are tallied. The five ideas with the most votes are then put up to a vote to determine the first-, second-, and third-best option.

## Norms

Norms (normative behavior) are the guidelines that dictate how members will treat each other, work together, and meet together when conducting the business of the group. Norms are developed as a group is formed and agreed to by every member of the group.

## P. I. D.

The P. I. D. procedure is used when seeking potential solutions using a creative/discovery process. When little or nothing is known about the problem or the solution, an imagination-based search strategy is employed. Three steps are employed in P. I. D. process.

Perceiving. The group constructs the 5Ws by using metaphors, archetypes, or creative brainstorming. Based on the associations made through the use of those creative instruments, the elements of the problem are recognized and identified.

Imaging. The group imagines the "end state" using techniques like scenario building, future search, future-scaping, or imagineering. The image created by the use of these strategies portrays the solution needed (the Dream phase of the 4Ds).

Design. Using an inductive approach, such as trial and error, elements of the solution are searched out or created to satisfy the solution criteria created from the image developed in Step 2. A creative search process is conducted until a solution or viable solutions are produced.

## PAAR

PAAR stands for plan, assign, assess, and review. It is a four-step process allowing stakeholders to actively manage the implementation of a solution.

Typically, leadership, or a subgroup of the stakeholders, are designated to the PAAR task.

The timeframe for carrying out a PAAR varies. A brief description of each of the four steps in the PAAR process is as follows:

Plan. A plan is a written strategy listing the who, what, where, when, why, and how the solution is to be accomplished. The plan contains the action to be completed, key people involved, lead person, resources required, expected outcome, anticipated timeframe, and completion date.

Assign. Appropriate personnel and leadership are selected, and allocation of appropriate resources is scheduled to accomplish the task.

Assess. Develop and implement a comprehensive two-pronged evaluation design. The design should be summative, judging whether a desired outcome has been reached. It is also should be formative, an evaluation that assesses progress and provides feedback for the purpose of redirecting resources and work to reach the intended goal.

Review. The review process is a series of observations and analyses that lead to a discrepancy analysis on the progress of solution implementation. Each episode assesses what is being done, whether it is meeting the standards of the criteria set, and if not, the appropriate course of action to take to make remediation adjustments.

## Post-its

A Post-it note (sticky note) is a small piece of paper with an adhesive on its back, made for temporarily attaching notes to documents and other surfaces.

## Problem-Solving Process

The Problem-Solving Process is a conscious act where an individual or group chooses to engage in a rational process of inquiry to examine, analyze, deliberate, and make a reasoned decision addressing a situation in need of resolution.

### Prouds and Sorrys

This is a simple technique for team member reflection and premeditative action. Members reflect on their meeting performance at the personal and role level. They consider the things they are proud of and those things they are sorry they did or neglected to do. *Prouds and Sorrys* is a way to create responses that define and describe what has been done in a meeting.

## Scenario

A written outline of the story, giving the details of the plot and individual scenes; a sequence or development of events.

## Scenario-Building Procedure

In the context of problem-solving, scenarios are constructed stories about the future, each one modeling a distinct, plausible worldview of future events. Following procedures are based upon the work of Jim Ogilvy and Peter Schwartz. Scenario building is developed in seven steps.

1. Select the focus point for the scenario. Identify the key issue or decision and the future context in which it exists. Develop a clear understanding of useful questions to ask about what that future might be. Determine the timeframe of the scenario based on the context of the scenario.

2. Determine the key forces that influence the organization's success or failure regarding the issue at hand. How have these forces (drivers) acted in the past? How are these forces patterned? How might they act in the future?

3. Compile available data about those people, places, and things that will drive the future and affect the direction of the outcome. From the data and trends, brainstorm a list of key factors that serve as the future drivers that will affect the direction outcome of the issue.

4. Prioritize the future drivers by the degree of uncertainty and degree of importance they might have. How do these identified drivers and trends affect the course of the scenario? Determine which factors are up for grabs and which of those are predetermined or inevitable.

5. Choose two or three of the key factors found that will be most critical in determining the future of the focal issue; make sure that the most powerful inevitabilities and uncertainties are accounted for.

6. Build a scenario. Create a plot for the story using two or three key factors identified in the previous step. Use other identified factors as subplots. Make the key local forces identified in the second step and the stakeholders of the organization the major and minor characters of the story. Have the story unfold from beginning to end.

7. Four scenarios should be built. They are the official case, preferred case, worst case, and best case.

## Skilled Discussion

A skillful discussion is a collaborative conversation with a purpose. It is conducted to build shared meaning, gain common agreement, analyze and evaluate, or make a decision.

### Snow Cards

*Snow Cards* is a Group Organizing technique used to generate ideas or options. The purpose of the activity is to be able to display group ideas and categorize ideas that are similar. It allows members of the group to thoughtfully gain a better understanding of an issue and voice their opinion in a nonthreatening manner. Here's how it works:

- Group leader presents the issue under consideration.
- Each participant is given one to five index cards and instructed to write one response regarding the issue per card. The group is given enough time to thoughtfully consider the responses.
- Members then write each of the responses on a 5 × 8 index card. Cards are then posted on a wall or flipcharts.

- Group members seek to clarify each of the ideas posted to gain shared understanding.

- Ideas are then rearranged by similarity or by some predefined identifier—such as strengths, weaknesses, opportunities, or threats.

- Each classification is reviewed by the group for clarification, winnowing, and consensus to produce the final list.

## Solution Criteria

Solution criteria are the standards by which a judgment or decision can be made. They should be clear, understandable, relative, fair and reasonable, and finally, realistic. They should be the yardsticks that accurately measure the elements of a successful solution.

### Spend-a-Dot

*Spend-a-Dot.* is a Group Organizer used to prioritize or rank a group of ideas or options. It can also be used as a voting method.

- Begin by posting solution options or ideas on a flipchart or a large piece of paper. Give each participant an equally allotted number of stick-on dots, usually 5 to 10 in number.

- Instruct each group member to place one or more dots next to the choices they prefer. Each member in turn votes their dots.

- Once all members have voted, count and tally the number of dots for each option.

- Discuss the results with the group.

## Stakeholders

Stakeholders are individuals or groups having a vested interest in the issue at hand in that they can affect the action or outcome of the issue or be affected by it. Stakeholders can be both internal and external to the organization. Internal stakeholders are directly involved in the input, through put, or output of the organization. External stakeholders are recipients of the actions and outcomes of the organization and are not directly involved.

### Straw Polling

*Straw polling* is a multipurpose Group Organizer. Its primary use is for a process check to determine where the group is on a particular issue or process. By being able to visually determine where members of the group stand on the issue, a facilitator can quickly get a sense of progress toward consensus or favorability of an idea. Here's the way it works:

- Suggest to the group that a straw poll is in order and gain group agreement.

- State the issue under review as a statement for agreement or disagreement, allow clarification, and ensure group members have a common understanding of the issue.

- Do a thumbs-up/thumbs-down vote.

- If the group has agreement, move forward with the process. If the group disagrees, backup and reframe. If the group is split, move to further clarification and discussion.

## SWOT

The *SWOT* (strengths, weaknesses, opportunities, and threats) analysis is an analytical framework used to assess the organization's ability to respond to a situation or issue in need of resolution. The principal use of the *SWOT* is to focus the group on determining the strengths, weaknesses, opportunities, and threats the issue under consideration presents. The *SWOT* asks the group to analyze and assess the internal and external factors supporting or preventing a successful outcome. Here are the steps for conducting a *SWOT*:

- Place four large charts on a wall or walls visible to all participants. Label each chart with one of the four headings: strengths, weaknesses, opportunities, and threats.

- In a small group setting, have each member review the situation and develop responses for each category. Responses are placed on $3 \times 5$ cards or sticky notes. Members complete and post their responses on the appropriate charts until the entire group completes the task. A clarification session is facilitated with the group. The implications of the SWOT are determined.

- In large groups, divide participants into four subgroups. Each subgroup is assigned one of the four charts. The groups use a brainstorming process and record their ideas. After an assigned amount of time, groups rotate to the next chart, and brainstorming continues recording new ideas on the chart. This process continues until all groups have had input on the four charts. Once completed, the subgroups conduct a gallery walk, studying the completed contents of each chart. The group then discusses the implications of what has been recorded.

## T-Chart

The *T-chart* is a Group Organizer used to elicit the either/or of an issue, principally looking at the pluses and minuses or the pros and cons. The *T-chart* can also be used to pinpoint a definition by describing what an idea is and is not. The procedure for using a *T-chart* is as follows:

- Using a large sheet of paper or a flipchart sheet, draw a horizontal line across the top of the page and a vertical line from the center of the horizontal line down to the bottom of the page. Write the opposing titles on either side of the centerline at the top of the page.

- State the issue under consideration by the group and provide reflection time to consider the pros and cons, pluses and minuses, or advantages and disadvantages of the issue.

- Using a round-robin process, have group members record their responses on the appropriate side of the chart.

- Once completed, have the group discuss the case for and the case against and its implications.

## Thumbs-Up, Thumbs-Down

*Thumbs-Up, Thumbs-Down* is a quick way to get a vote on an issue. Thumbs-up means a group member approves of the issue under consideration. Thumbs-down means the group member disapproves of the issue under consideration. Thumbs-sideways means the group member has no opinion or is neutral on the subject.

## Whip Around Process

*The Whip Around Process* is a quick way of getting responses from a group. It could be used as a check for understanding, to assess the temperament of the group, or as a brainstorming procedure. Here's how it works:

- Facilitator asks the question or provides a declaratory statement.

- Group members reflect on the topic for a designated amount of time.

- The group leader asks the group members to respond, starting at one end of the table and working to the other end. Members respond in turn. Members can pass, if they are not ready to respond. The rounds continue until all members have had their say. Responses are recorded either on a flipchart or a chart paper.

## Winnowing

*Winnowing* is a process used to clarify and refine an idea or concept. By eliminating duplicates, combining ideas, and eliminating stray ideas, the group constructs a definition. *Winnowing* is a three-step process of discussion, modification, and consensus.

# For Further Reading

The texts selected here are meant to assist the reader in his or her quest to learn more about leading workgroups in problem solving. They do not represent the latest narratives on their subject. They were chosen because they are seminal texts on the subject or due to their practical applicability. Some will discuss the theory and practice in depth. Others will provide "tricks of the trade"—strategies, tactics, and tools that can be immediately used by the reader. The texts presented are organized into five categories: facilitation, groups and teams, meeting essentials, problem solving, and major problem-solving strategies. Each title is followed by a short annotation that thumbnails what the book is about and how it might be used.

This is a starter bibliography. Hopefully, the reader will scan through one or more of these texts and become more interested in its contents, providing the motivation to dig even deeper. The more you learn the better you will lead. The subject matter dealing with groups of people trying to problem solve is not a matter of a text or two but the subject of many academic disciplines. This bibliography provides a modest beginning on a road to a great adventure. Have fun learning.

## Facilitation

**Bens, I. (2000). *Facilitating with ease: A step-by-step guidebook*. John Wiley & Sons.**

A perfect starter book for anyone new to facilitation. Bens takes a neophyte on a step-by-step journey through the process of facilitation while teaching the competencies for being a successful facilitator. This book mentors the reader through the stages and process of facilitation, Specific chapters are dedicated to understanding group participants, facilitating participation, managing conflict, leading decision-making, and meeting management. The final two chapters are dedicated to process tools (GOs) and meeting process designs. The text is ideal for the beginner.

The first four chapters should be read in toto and studied in preparation for a facilitation responsibility. The remaining chapters can be consulted as needed, based on their subject matter.

**Kaner, S., Lind, L., Toldi, C., Fisk, F., & Berger, D. (2014). *Facilitator's guide to participatory decision-making* (3rd ed.). Jossey-Bass.**

This internationally acclaimed text is the gold standard for managing and facilitating decision-making groups. It is the consultant's guide to leading groups and presents a master class in collaborative decision-making processes. The emphasis of the text is on the participatory aspects of the process. Divided into five parts, Kaner presents a detailed conversation on the grounding principles of participatory decision-making, the fundamentals of facilitation, the nature of sustainable agreements, facilitating sustainable agreements, and reaching closure. Complex ideas in a very simple way through the use of graphics and outlines. This text is on the bookshelf of every journeyman facilitator.

This is a must-read for anyone interested in understanding the complexities of leading and facilitating a collaborative group.

**Rees, F. (2005). *The facilitator excellence handbook*. Pfeiffer.**

Rees has written a comprehensive guide covering the skills, tasks, and knowledge required of an effective facilitator and presents the competencies necessary to attain them. The text is an excellent guide for honing facilitative skills and learning to facilitate difficult situations. Divided into five parts, she defines facilitation, basic facilitation skills, facilitation methods and tools, effective meeting designs, and facilitating in various venues. This is the how-to book for those who facilitate regularly.

The reader should approach this book as a competency guide, using it when preparing for a facilitation and as a checkpoint to evaluate facilitation performance.

**Schwarz, R. (2002). *The skilled facilitator* (2nd ed.). Jossey-Bass.**

The seminal text on facilitation, this comprehensive text is required reading for anyone who is facilitating or consulting professionally. For those who are collaborative leaders, who desire to improve on their skills and techniques for working with groups, this is a required read as well. The text is divided into five parts: Part 1, how facilitation helps groups; Part 2, diagnosing group behavior; Part 3, group intervention skills; Part 4, agreeing to work with groups and cofacilitators; Part 5, using facilitation in your own organization. This read is a must for anyone who wants to understand facilitation in depth.

This book is not a casual read. It is meant to be studied. Note-taking and discussing the content with others works well. The text can also be consulted topically to gain a comprehensive understanding of the subject presented.

**Strachan, D. (2007). *Making questions work: A guide to what and how to ask for facilitators, consultants, managers, coaches and educators*. Jossey-Bass.**

Questioning is the language of the facilitator. How a question is asked and phrased can make or break a facilitation. Strachan has compiled a text of questions for all facilitative occasions. This highly practical work is divided into two parts. Part 1 defines and describes the "nuts and bolts" of effective questioning. Part 2 details the processes and strategies for questioning in specific meeting situations. This is another text that is on the bookshelf of the practicing facilitator. A reader who wants to improve her or his communication skills should read and study Part 1 of the book. It defines and describes the basics of effective questioning.

Part 2 is an ideal reference to use when preparing to facilitate.

**Weaver, R. G., & Farrell, J. D. (1999).** *Managers as facilitators: A practical guide to getting work done in a changing workspace.* **Berrett-Kohler.**

Collaborative leaders facilitate change. This text provides guidance to leaders who want to learn how to lead and create a participatory environment in workgroups. Part 1 addresses the essentials of facilitation management. This part emphasizes the roles and skillsets of the manager/leader in setting the charter, facilitating development, and managing a workgroup. Part 2 addresses the role of facilitation in managing group boundaries and change. This is a must-read for the collaborative leader.

As the title states, this is a guide. The text covers the major situations leaders face when working with groups. Topically organized, it can be read and studied based on the situation confronting the leader.

## Groups and Teams

**Dannemiller Tyson Associates. (2000).** *Whole–scale change toolkit.* **Berrett-Koehler.**

This high-powered group of business consultants has been facilitating large-scale organizational change in planning, culture building, and reorganization of major U.S. and international corporations since 1984. They are experts in facilitating large-group problem-solving processes. This toolkit let's you in on how they go about facilitating large-group sessions. It provides a template for a large-group action learning design that can be adapted to any normal situation. The first four chapters deal with planning, designing, leadership, facilitation, and logistics of a large-scale meeting. Each chapter includes a meeting script for leading the sessions about the chapter's topic. Chapter 5 lays out a generic three-day event plan and facilitation script. Chapter 6 provides examples of large-scale events addressing specific organizational topics. Again, each topic has a facilitation script and meeting outline. An actual exemplar case is also provided. Issues like strategic planning, restricting, and visioning are a few of the topics addressed.

To get a practical perspective for conducting a large-scale meeting, be it a monthly all-school event or a special issue meeting of all staff, read and learn the beginning chapters. This is a first resource to grab when planning a large-scale event. Reviewing the scripts, meeting sequences, assigned tasks, and facilitation strategies will provide an invaluable source of ideas and applications. The large-scale meeting doesn't have to be a yawner. Ford Auto Company and the Bank of America can't afford to have yawners. Check out what this book has to offer. It will be worth the time.

**Dyer, W. G. (1987).** *Team Building* **(2nd ed.). Addison-Wesley.**

This book was chosen because of its straightforward approach at developing a team. Dyer pioneered many of the strategies used in team development. While the strategies and examples are based in the business environment, the developmental sequence presented is spot on. This is a how-to-do-it book on team development. Part 1 defines teams and the concept of team development. Part 2 provides the strategies and tactics for building a team development program. Part 3 provides strategies for developing a new team, conflict managing teams, revitalizing teams, and dealing with inter-team conflicts. Part 4 deals with special issues, such as people problems in teams.

The reader can use this text's contents as a series of recipes in team development. The text was meant to provide guidance to consultants and managers whose job was to develop a team, and it is written in that fashion.

**Hunter, D., Bailey, A., & Taylor, B. (1995).** *The Zen of groups.* **Fisher Books.**

Don't let the title fool you. This is not a feel-good book. The authors are providing wisdom about groups in succinct kernels and nutshells. A handbook it is. Part 1 of the text covers the wide expanse of team leadership and team development using descriptive outlines to cover the topic. Part 2 is a toolkit of techniques and exercises topically arranged for immediate application in specific group situations. Toolkit entries are designed like the cue cards used in this text. Part 2 will extend your knowledge of Group Organizers, as well as provide new strategies for dealing with group dynamics.

Read the first part carefully. It won't take long. Reflect on each topic. These questions might help in your reflection. What did it say? What does it mean? How will it change what I think and do?

Part 2 is a go-to resource. When trying to confront a group situation, check the table of contents. There are group organizers, techniques, and exercises offered that can be immediately applied. While the toolbox doesn't cover everything, it's one of the desk resources to have when working with groups.

**Levi, D. (2016).** *Group dynamics for teams* **(5th ed.). Sage.**

This book is a favorite because it transfers theory to practice. Using the research and theory from group and social psychology, the author describes how to transfer the theory to practice. The text is not written for the academic but rather the leader practitioner interested in understanding how groups grow and function as teams. Divided into four parts, it covers team characteristics, team development and team processes, team make-up and special issues, and culture and team types. Each chapter explains the theory of its subject matter clearly and in layperson's terms. Each theoretical position is followed by the "how-to," putting the theory into practice. This book is a primer on the theory of practicing group development. It is a great first book in the study of group dynamics and team development.

This is a read-and-study book. Simply written, the concepts should become immediately apparent and the "reason for the madness" for much of what has been presented in the eight chapters of this text.

## Meeting Essentials

**Adams, J. L. (2019).** *Conceptual blockbusting: A guide to better ideas* **(5th ed.). Basic Books.**

Much of what problem solvers do is creative. Thinking creatively for individuals, let alone groups, is a difficult task. This is the seminal text for learning to generate creative ideas and how to think out-of-the-box. It is a must-read. The first six chapters of conceptual blockbusting identify the perceptual, emotional, cultural, environmental, intellectual, and expressive blocks preventing groups from thinking creatively. Chapters 6 and 7 describe the languages used and the techniques employed to blockbust stale thinking and break out into creative thinking. Chapters 8 and 9 deal with blockbusting in groups and organizations. The last chapter deals with creativity in the future. This book is a requirement for those who want to learn how to think out-of-the-box.

To fully comprehend the contents of this book, the reader should read for understanding, reflect on what is being read, and complete the exercises designed to assist in learning the material.

**Higgins, J. M. (2006).** *101 creative problem-solving techniques: The handbook of new ideas for business* **(Rev. ed.). New Management Publishing Company.**

This is the single-stop resource for group organizers. Our text is presented in a limited number of group organizers, also called structuring devices, and in this case, call techniques. Higgins has taken the time to compile all of the major group organizers in one text. The text begins with chapters on how to innovate and create in the problem-solving process. The rest of the text is a compendium of group organizers categorized by their use in certain situations. This is a must-have on the facilitator's bookshelf. An invaluable resource for engaging teams and organizing thinking, this text is used as a reference.

**Isaacs, W. (1999).** *Dialog and the art of thinking together.* **Doubleday.**

The ability to dialog is an essential skill that, if possessed, allows individuals and groups to be incredibly productive by being able to literally think together. For most of us, learning to be quiet, to actively listen, and to unconditionally respond in a conversation is an extremely hard thing to do, let alone applying these behaviors in groups, where it becomes exponentially more difficult. Those interested in workgroup dialog will find reading this seminal text a very rewarding resource. This book teaches a new way of being in a conversation with others. It is not meant to be used only in workgroups but offers a new way of being with others for all occasions. The book not only teaches the knowledge skills and techniques of dialog but also instructs the reader in the dispositions necessary to have any productive conversation. Anyone interested in dialog should read this text.

Read, contemplate, reflect; repeat. This text is a heavy hitter. Take the time to learn these ideas well, and you will be well rewarded.

**Morgan, G. (1997).** *Imaginization: New mindsets received, organizing, and managing.* **Berrett-Koehler.**

A critical step in the problem-solving process is successfully imaging a solution. One way of getting at these solution images is by metaphor, which is the subject of this text. Morgan uses different metaphors as mindscapes to look at various aspects of an organization. These mindscapes, such as spider plants, termites, or political footballs, can help groups image current and future conditions. His chapters on imaging teamwork and picturing power provide strong strategies for imaging as well. For those readers interested in exploring the creative aspects of imaging a solution, this book provides the answers.

Morgan writes in a vibrant style. Consequently, the text is a casual read.

**Senge, P., Kleiner, A., Roberts, C., Ross, R. B., & Smith, B. J. (1994).** *The fifth discipline field book: Strategies and tools for building a learning organization.* **Doubleday.**

This is a follow-up text to Peter Senge's groundbreaking text *The Fifth Discipline*, a prerequisite read for understanding this text. This field guide is its practical application. The field book is structured to follow the sequence of *The Fifth Discipline*. Each of the five disciplines has a chapter devoted to it. Each chapter provides the strategies, tactics, tools, and techniques supporting the development of that discipline. The team of writers provides a treasure trove of ideas and practical suggestions that are invaluable learning for the participatory leader. This is a truly great resource for facilitator leadership. Of particular note is the book's treatment of conducting skilled conversations and dialog. Both Richard Ross and Bill Isaac make comments here.

There are two strategies for reading this book. The first is to read and study for the purpose of learning practical ideas for becoming a collaborative leader. The second is using the text as a reference, particularly in studying modes of communication.

**Straus, D., & Doyle, M. (1976).** *How to make meetings work: The new interactive method.* **Berkeley Books.**

This is *the* seminal book on conducting participatory meetings. This is where the concepts of interactive meetings really started. Anyone who wants to know how to run a successful meeting must learn the contents of this book. If you are only going to read one book from this bibliography, read this one.

## Problem Solving

**Hayes, J. R. (1989).** *The complete problem solver* **(2nd ed.). Lawrence Erlbaum Associates.**

Those interested in understanding the psychology behind problem solving will find this text to be exceptionally informative. In addition to providing foundational theoretical knowledge about problem solving, this text describes the skills necessary to become a good problem solver. While it focuses on individuals problem solving, the information presented has great applications for leaders and groups. It is divided into four parts: problem-solving theory and practice, memory and knowledge acquisition, decision-making, and creativity and invention. Each part covers salient topics such as learning strategies and decision-making methods. This is an academic theory and practice book.

The reader should approach this book as if he or she were taking independent study class on the subject. Study the text as if you will be taking a final examination. Only in this case, there's no teacher, nor final. The real final here is your ability to understand and apply the concepts presented in real time on main street.

**Nutt, P. C. (1990).** *Making tough decisions: Tactics for improving managerial Decision-making.* **Jossey-Bass.**

This book is a seminal text on decision-making and problem solving from an alternate universe. Paul's text is an academic tome that covers the aspects of decision-making and problem solving in a comprehensive fashion for managers and executives in the business community. If the reader really wants to understand the fundamentals of problem solving and decision-making, this book will provide most of the answers. It's not meant for the faint of heart. It is the type of read one would expect to see in an advanced executive leadership course of study.

Reading this book requires a certain amount of academic discipline. Putting the effort into this text will provide a wealth of invaluable knowledge. Sometimes, you get out of something what you put into it, and this is one of those cases.

**Sternberg, R. J. (Ed.). (1998).** *Thinking and problem solving: Handbook of perception and cognition* **(2nd ed.). Academic Press.**

This book was selected for its treatise on the theoretical foundations of problem solving and thinking. It is an academic handbook, presenting an in-depth discussion on thirteen topics, each addressed by experts in that area. The following are the topic areas: *The History of Research on Thinking and Problem-Solving, Contemporary Approaches to the Study of Thinking and Problem Solving, Knowledge Representation, Concepts and Categories, Deduction and Its Cognitive Basis, Inductive Reasoning, Problem-Solving, Language and Thought, Intelligence, Creativity, Development of Problem-Solving, Cultural Dimensions of Cognition: Complex Dynamic System of Constraints and Possibilities,* and *The Teaching and Thinking of Problem-Solving.*

Since this is a handbook; it should be used as a reference to dig deep into the topics presented.

## Major Problem-Solving Strategies

**Bryson, J. M., & Alston, F. K (2011).** *Creating and implementing your strategic plan: A workbook for profit and nonprofit organizations.* **Jossey-Bass.**

This workbook is a companion to Bryson's seminal work on strategic planning, *Strategic Planning for Public and Nonprofit Organizations.* As with the *Fifth Discipline Field Book,* this text outlines the practical applications based on the Bryson model. It covers all the bases from readiness to implementation in a straightforward and simple fashion, and it is divided into two parts. Part 1 is an overview of strategic planning and the implementation process; Part 2 covers each of the 10 steps of the Bryson strategic-planning process in detail. This is a great guide for the problem solver new to the strategic-planning process.

This is a guidebook and should be used as such. Particularly noteworthy are the worksheets that can be used to help design and implement strategic-planning sessions.

**Burnett, J. (2002).** *Managing business crises: From anticipation to implementation.* **Quorum Books.**

This book is closely aligned to the 3 Cs crisis model from the text. It provides detailed descriptions and explanations of how to deal with all phases of a crisis. While it is targeted to the business audience, it's strategies tactics and techniques are very much applicable to school settings. It is an easy read and provides the background information to be able to fully understand how to prepare and handle a catastrophic event. It is definitely a go-to book.

**Cornish, E. (2005).** *Futuring: The exploration of the future.* **World Future Society.**

Much of the thinking that goes into imaging a solution relies on the ability to image the future. Edward Cornish presents this groundbreaking text on the subject of futuring—the ability to see the future to anticipate needs, obstacles, and solutions. In this text, Corish takes the reader through the trends that affect the future, how change occurs, futuring methods, scenario building, and ways of inventing and predicting the future. The content in this book provides the reader with the practical ways to image the solution. A must-read for the creative problem solver.

Futuring is not a how-to text but more of a what-to-do text and should be read accordingly.

**Kepner, C., & Tregoe, B. (1997). *The new rational manager*. Kepner-Tregoe.**

Our text's seven-step model is based on the concepts of Kepner and Tregoe. The book *The New General Rational Manager* provides the foundational elements for the seven-step model. While *The New Rational Manager* text is directed to the business community, it's nine chapters provide detailed descriptions and explanations for a rational problem-solving process. Anyone wanting to build a strong foundational understanding of group rational problem solving will find this seminal text will be of great assistance.

**Weisbord, M., & Janoff, S. (2000). *Future search: An Action guide to finding common ground in organizations and communities* (2nd ed.). Berrett–Kohler.**

The Future Search Conference is a large group-meeting process used to do strategic planning or conducted in tandem with a strategic-planning process. It can also be used as a large-group strategy to image a solution. The text provides this well-defined process and the steps that allow an individual not only to understand the concepts of strategic planning but to actually apply them in real time. The book is divided into three sections: Section 1 explains the concepts of future search and how to design a future search meeting. Section 2 provides direction on the planning, facilitating, and after conference activities necessary to conduct a successful future search conference. Section 3 provides appendices on the various resources needed to carry out a future search conference. This text is used as a guide.

# Bibliography

Adams, J. L. (2019). *Conceptual blockbusting: A guide to better ideas* (5th ed.). Basic Books.
Argyris, C., Putnam, R., & Smith McLain, D. (1985). *Action science*. Jossey Bass.
Argyris, C., & Schon, D. (1974). *Theory in practice: Increasing professional effectiveness*. Jossey-Bass.
Bens, I. (2000). *Facilitating with ease: A step-by-step guidebook*. John Wiley and Sons.
Booth, C., Columb, G., & Williams, J. (2016). *The craft of research*. University of Chicago Press.
Bryson, J. (1996). *Creating and implementing your strategic plan: A workbook for profit and nonprofit organizations*. Jossey-Bass.
Burnett, J. (2002). *Managing business crises: From anticipation to implementation*. Quorum Books.
Cornish, E. (2005). *Futuring: The exploration of the future*. World Future Society.
Dannemiller Tyson Associates. (2000). *Whole–scale change toolkit*. Berrett-Koehler.
Dewey, J. (1997). *How we think*. Dover Publications.
Dyer, W. G. (1987). *Team building* (2nd ed.). Addison-Wesley.
Goldhammer, J. (1996). *Under the influence*. Prometheus.
Hayes, J. R. (1989). *The complete problem solver* (2nd ed.). Lawrence Erlbaum Associates.
Higgins, J. M. (2006). *101 Creative problem-solving techniques: The handbook of new ideas for business* (Rev. ed.). New Management Publishing Company.
Hunter, D., Bailey, A., & Taylor, B. (1995). *The Zen of groups*. Fisher Books.
Isaacs, W. (1999). *Dialogue and the art of thinking together*. Doubleday.
Joiner, B., & Josephs, S. (2007). *Leadership agility: Five levels of mastery for anticipating and initiating change*. Jossey-Bass.
Kaner, S. (2014). *Facilitator's guide to participatory decision-making* (3rd ed.). Jossey-Bass.
Katzenbach, J., & Smith, D. (1994). *The wisdom of teams: Creating the high performance organization*. Harper Business.
Kepner, C., & Tregoe, B. (1997). *The new rational manager*. Kepner-Tregoe.
Knutson, J., & Alexander, L. (1981). *Contingency planning*. Education for Management.
Kurtz, C. F., & Snowden, D. J. (2003). The new dynamics of strategy: Sense-making in a complex and complicated world. *IBM Systems Journal, 42*(3), 462–483. https://doi.org/10.1147/sj.423.0462
Lencioni, P. (2004). *Death by meeting*. Jossey-Bass.
Levi, D. (2001). *Group dynamics for teams*. Sage.
Lyles, R. I. (1982). *Practical management problem solving and decision making*. Van Nostrand Reinhold Company.
Marquardt, M. J. (2018). *Optimizing the power of action learning: Real-time Strategies for developing leaders, building teams, and transforming organizations* (3rd. ed.). Nicholas Brealey Publishing.
Morgan, G. (1997a). *Images of organization*. SAGE.
Morgan, G. (1997b). *Imaginization: New mindsets received, organizing, and managing*. Berrett-Koehler.
Nutt, P. C. (1990). *Making tough decisions: Tactics for improving managerial decision-making*. Jossey-Bass.
Pokras, S. (1995). *Team problem solving*. Viability Group.
Proctor, T. (2010). *Creative problem solving for managers* (3rd ed.). Routledge.
Rees, F. (2005). *The facilitator excellence handbook*. Pfeiffer.
Schwartz, P. (1996). *The art of the long view*. Doubleday.

Schwarz, R. (2002). *The skilled facilitator* (2nd ed.). Jossey-Bass.
Senge, P. (1990). *The fifth discipline: The art and practice of the learning organization.* Doubleday.
Senge, P. (1994). *The fifth discipline field book: Strategies and tools for building a learning organization.* Doubleday.
Sternberg, R. J. (Ed.). (1998). *Thinking and problem solving: Handbook of perception and cognition* (2nd ed.). Academic Press.
Strachan, D. (2007). *Making questions work: A guide to what and how to ask for facilitators, consultants, managers, coaches and educators.* Jossey Bass.
Straus, D., & Doyle, M. (1976). *How to make meetings work: The new interactive method.* Berkeley Books.
Tagliere, D. A. (1992). *How to meet, think, and work to consensus.* Pfeiffer.
Toulmin, S., Rieke, R., & Janik, A. (1984). *An introduction to reasoning* (2nd ed.). Macmillan.
Weaver, R. G., & Farrell, J. D. (1999). *Managers as facilitators: A practical guide to getting work done in a changing workspace.* Berrett-Kohler.
Weisbord, M. R., & Janoff, S. (2000). *Future search: An action guide to finding common ground in organizations and communities* (2nd ed.). Berrett-Kohler.
Wycoff, J. (1995). *Transformational thinking.* The Berkeley Publishing Co.

# Index

Action learning, 80–81, 80 (figure), 96, 154
Action plans, 154
Administrivia, 120, 154
   problems, 19
Assessment process, 127–130
Assign resources, 120, 123, 126–127

Blue skying, 60 (figure), 96, 154
Booth, Wayne, 23
Brainstorming, 12, 23, 24, 41, 93, 154–155, 161, 162, 166–167
Break territorial silos, 43
Bulldozer, 105

Changing problems, 27–28
Chaotic problems, 29–30, 83–84
Chicken Little, 57
Clarification process, 155
Collaboration, 7, 8–9, 37, 106, 135, 141
Collaborative leadership, 8
Columb, Gregory, 22
Common understanding and intent
   Foibles and Fumbles, 36–38
   problem understanding, 51–52
   stakeholders, 39–42
   stakeholders' commitment to work together, 42–50
Communication modes, 133, 141
Complex problem, 29
Complicated problem, 29
Conference Crusaders, 56
Confront clicks/cabals, 43
Consensus process, 156
Contingency planning, 155–156
Cooperative workgroup, 8
Crisis management plan, 156–157
Cub Scouts, 45
Cynefin Framework, 27

Dark-colored circles, 40
Decide on the solution, 116–117
   Foibles and Fumbles, 104–106
Decision-making process, 2, 5–7, 9, 11, 73, 92, 104, 106–108, 142
   Foibles and Fumbles, 104–106

Deck chairs, 43
Deficiency, 21, 24, 25, 60, 103
Deficit, 24, 60–61, 79
Demographics, 25
Descriptive rubric, 109, 113, 113 (figure), 157
Desired state, 59–64
Dialog, 145–147, 156–157
Differentiating, 157
Difficult problems, 1
Discrepancy analysis, 58–59, 58 (figure), 157
Divine right of kings, 104–105
4Ds, 158–159
Dyads and triads, 157–158

Elephant hunting, 43
Eliminate cultural blocks, 43
Emerging opportunity, 24–25
Emotional problem, 2
Epilogue, 122

Farrell, J. D., 44
Formal problem-solving processes, 8
Formative evaluation process, 127–129, 128 (figure), 158

Gallery walk, 159
Gap analysis, 159
Glossary terms, 134
Goldhammer, John, 44
Group organizers, 12, 23, 134, 159
Group size, 134

High school leadership council, 25
Humphrey, Albert, 31
Hysterics, 57

Imaging, 55–58, 162. *See also* Solution, imaging
Insiders group, 51

Kindergarten teachers, 21
Kurtz, Cynthia, 27

Lencioni, Pat, 11
Levi, Dan, 44

Maslow, Abraham, 12
Meeting
   accordion process, 149–151
   agenda, 137
   basic setting, 151, 151 (figure)
   beginning, 135
   collaborative participant, 142–144
   conducting, 138
   dialog conducting, 145–147
   ending, 135–136
   facilitator, 137–138
   Flipchart, 139
   large group settings, 152–153, 152 (figure)
   large-sized group meeting procedures, 147–149
   manager, 136
   medium-sized group meeting procedures, 147
   playbook, 134
   process observer, 139–142
   recorder, 138–139
   roles, 133, 134
   skillful discussion conducting, 144–145
   small-group meeting procedures, 147
   space, 134
Mind mapping, 160
Mindscaping, 160–161

NBA players, 45
Newbies, 51
Next steps, 131–132
Nominal group technique, 161
Norms, 162
Nutt, Paul, 51

PAAR. *See* Plan, assign, assess, and review (PAAR)
Performance review, 131
P. I. D. procedure, 162
Plan, assign, assess, and review (PAAR), 124–125, 125 (figure), 162–163
Pokras, Sandy, 51
Pope, Alexander, 19
Post-it note (sticky note), 163
Problems
   defining, 18–21
   description of, 32
   difficulty of, 27–30, 27 (figure), 30
   elements of, 21–24, 23 (figure)
   Foibles and Fumbles, 18–21
   potency and urgency of, 31–32

SWOT analysis, 31–32, 31 (figure)
type of, 24–27, 24 (figure)
workplace problem, 21, 21 (figure)
written definition, 32–33
Problem-solver's toolbox, 14
   action learning, 154
   action plans, 154
   administrivia, 154
   blue skying, 154
   brainstorming, 154–154
   clarification process, 155
   communication modes, 133
   consensus process, 155
   contingency planning, 155–156
   crisis management plan, 156–157
   descriptive rubric, 115
   dialog, 156–157
   differentiating, 157
   discrepancy analysis process, 157
   4Ds, 158–161
   dyads and triads, 157–158
   formative evaluation, 158
   gallery walk, 159
   gap analysis, 157
   glossary terms, 134
   group organizers, 26, 52, 62, 147
   group size, 134
   imaging, 160
   meeting. *See* Meeting
   meeting playbook, 133
   meeting roles, 133
   meeting space, 134
   mind mapping, 160
   mindscaping, 160–161
   nominal group technique, 161
   norms, 162
   PAAR, 162–163
   P. I. D. procedure, 162
   post-it note (sticky note), 163
   problem-solving process, 163
   prouds and sorrys, 163
   scenario-building procedure, 163–164
   skilled discussion, 164
   snow cards, 164–165
   solution criteria, 165
   spend-a-dot, 165
   stakeholders, 165
   straw polling, 165–166
   SWOT analysis, 166
   T-Chart, 167

thumbs-down, 167
thumbs-up, 167
whip around process, 167
winnowing, 168
Problem-solving procedure
    chaotic problems, 83–85
    complex problems, 82–83
    complicated problems, 81–82
    Foibles and Fumbles, 70
    simple problems, 80–81
Problem-solving process, 165
    assessment process, 127–130
    assign resources, 126–127
    Foibles and Fumbles, 120–124
    review progress, 130–132
    solution plan, 125–126, 126 (figure)
Problem solving, schools
    collaborative leader, 9–10
    collaborative problem solving, 3
    collaborative process, 7–8
    cooperative workgroup, 10
    emotional problem solving, 2
    formal problem-solving
        structures, 12
    leadership foibles and fumbles, 13–14
    organized text, 14
    rational problem solving, 3
    sound meeting structures, 10–11
    stakeholders, 6
    successful collaboration, prerequisites for, 8
Procrastinators, 14
Progress loops, 130 (figure)
Prouds and sorrys, 163
Psychic prison, 122

Rating system and evaluate alternatives,
    108–115
    criteria and solution documentation sheet,
        109 (figure)
    descriptive rubric, 113–115, 113 (figure)
    Foibles and Fumbles, 104–105
    simple counting, 109, 110 (figure)
    solution criteria performance, 110 (figure)–
        113 (figure)
    weighted ranking, 109, 112 (figure)
Rational problem, 2
Review meeting, elements of, 131–132
Review progress, 130–131
Rieke, Richard D., 22
Righteous ideologues, 14

Saxe, John Godfrey, 22
Scenario, 163
Scenario-building procedure, 163–164
Schwarz, R., 44
Search strategies
    defining, 91–92
    experiment-based searches, 92–93
    Foibles and Fumbles, 88–90
    imagination-based searches, 93
    knowledge-based searches, 91–92
    tit for tat, 90
    Tug-of-War, 90
Sequential improvement, 25, 61
Seven step problem-solving process,
    3–6, 3 (figure)
*Seventeens*, 55
Sharing airtime, 48
Shoehorners, 55–56
Simon, Herb, 121
Simple counting, 110 (figure), 111
Simple problem, 28
Skilled discussion, 142, 164
*Skilled Facilitator*, 44
Snow cards, 164–165
Snowden, Dave, 27
Solution alternatives
    action learning, 96
    contingency planning, 96–97
    creative problem solving, 97
    crisis management, 97–99
    Foibles and Fumbles, 88–90
    formula for searching for, 94 (figure)
    four cases, 95–101
Solution criteria, 167
    criteria building, keeping tabs on, 76–79
    developing criteria, 75–76
    Foibles and Fumbles, 70
    performance, 110 (figure)
    solution alternatives, 72
    solution criteria, 73–74
    *Turducken*, 71–72
    warm fuzzy, 70
Solution, imaging
    Chicken Little, 57
    desired state, 59–65
    discrepancy analysis, 58–59, 58 (figure)
    Foibles and Fumbles, 55–57
    research, 56–57
    *Seventeens*, 55
    shoehorners, 55–56

solution impact, 65–67
Solution impact, 65–67
Solution plan, 125–126, 125 (figure)
   checklist, 126 (figure)
Solution reviews, 131
Sound meeting structures, 10–12
Sound problem-solving meetings, 11
Spend-a-dot, 165
*Spockeans*, 105
Stakeholders, 39–42, 165
Standard school meeting, 11
Static problems, 27
Sticky note. *See* Post-it note
Straw polling, 165–166
Summative evaluation, 129–130
Surface personal vendettas and squabbles, 43
SWOT analysis, 166

T-Chart, 167
Thumbs-down, 167
Thumbs-up, 167
Toolbox, 14
Toulmin, Stephen, 22
Transformational thinking, 60

Vantage points, 22

Weaver, R. G., 44
Weighted ranking, 112, 112 (figure)
Whip around process, 167
Williams, Jamie, 35
Williams, Joseph, 35
Winnowing, 168
Workplace problem, 2
Work presentation, 131

# CORWIN
A Sage Company

**Helping educators make the greatest impact**

**CORWIN HAS ONE MISSION:** to enhance education through intentional professional learning.

We build long-term relationships with our authors, educators, clients, and associations who partner with us to develop and continuously improve the best evidence-based practices that establish and support lifelong learning.

# Solutions YOU WANT | Experts YOU TRUST | Results YOU NEED

### INSTITUTES

Corwin Institutes provide regional and virtual events where educators collaborate with peers and learn from industry experts. Prepare to be recharged and motivated!

**corwin.com/institutes**

### ON-SITE PROFESSIONAL LEARNING

Corwin on-site PD is delivered through high-energy keynotes, practical workshops, and custom coaching services designed to support knowledge development and implementation.

**www.corwin.com/pd**

### VIRTUAL PROFESSIONAL LEARNING

Our virtual PD combines live expert facilitation with the flexibility of anytime, anywhere professional learning. See the power of intentionally designed virtual PD.

**www.corwin.com/virtualworkshops**

### CORWIN ONLINE

Online learning designed to engage, inform, challenge, and inspire. Our courses offer practical, classroom-focused instruction that will meet your continuing education needs and enhance your practice.

**www.corwinonline.com**

Visit www.corwin.com

CORWIN